FRO HEREFO
THREE COCKS , ᵣ ᵢᵤ ᵢᵢᵤN

THE HEREFORD, HAY AND BRECON RAILWAY

by
John Mair

A two-coach train is standing in the down (left-hand) platform road. In the distance an engine appears to have just used, or is about to use, the crossover between the down and up lines. The coaches standing on the up line west of the station appear to have been stranded! Note the signals at the end of the down platform. The upper arm is the starting signal, and the lower is the distant signal for Eardisley West. The white markings on the arms seem to be stripes rather than circles, and if so, the picture would have been taken after 1906. *John Alsop collection*

THE OAKWOOD PRESS

© John Mair, 2021

ISBN 978-0-85361-750-1

Printed by
Blissetts, Roslin Road, Acton, W3 8DH

For
Julianna

A staged photograph, which was later turned into a postcard and annotated, of four trains
at Three Cocks Junction. *John Alsop collection*

Front cover: On a wet day an eastbound train enters Whitney-on-the-Wye station. Note the
impressive, and typical, Midland Railway (MR) running-in name board.

John Alsop collection

Published by
The Oakwood Press, 54-58 Mill Square, Catrine, KA5 6RD
Telephone: 01290 551122   Website: www.stenlake.co.uk

Contents

One   **Historical Outline** **7**

The Hay and Kington Railways 7, Proposals for new railways 8, The Hereford, Hay and Brecon Railway 11, Access to Hereford 13, Construction of the Hereford, Hay and Brecon Railway 18, Gradients 20, Train services begin 21, Amalgamation and Separation with the Brecon and Merthyr Railway 22, Enter the Midland Railway 23, Swansea Vale; and Neath and Brecon 25, Leasing and purchase of the HH&BR 27, The Kington and Eardisley Railway 27, The Golden Valley Railway 28, The absentee London and North Western Railway 29, The Midland in charge 30, Access to Barrs Court Station 32, Improvements 34, The First World War 35, The Return of Peace 35, The Grouping 36, The inter-war years 36, No Halts – or Railcars 38, The Second World War 39, Peace again ... and Nationalization 40, The ICI Trains 41, Closure 42

Two   **Operating the Line** **51**

The Midland in charge 52, Passenger services 52, Changing at Three Cocks Junction 56, By train to school 58, Goods trains 59, The ICI trains 61, Local goods traffic again 62, Motive power 63, Passenger Rolling stock 68, Goods rolling stock 70, Signalling 70, *Hereford* 72, *Credenhill* 72, *Moorhampton and Kinnersley* 76, *Eardisley Junction and Eardisley West; Whitney-on-Wye* 78, *Hay Junction and Hay Station* 80, *Glasbury-on-Wye* 82, *Three Cocks Junction* 82, Signals 84, Speed Restrictions 86, Station facilities for passengers 86

Three   **A Journey from Hereford in Later Years** **87**

Epilogue **101**

Bibliography **103**

Index **104**

General view, looking east. Large MR nameboard 'WHITNEY-ON-THE-WYE', c. 1910.

Tony Harden collection

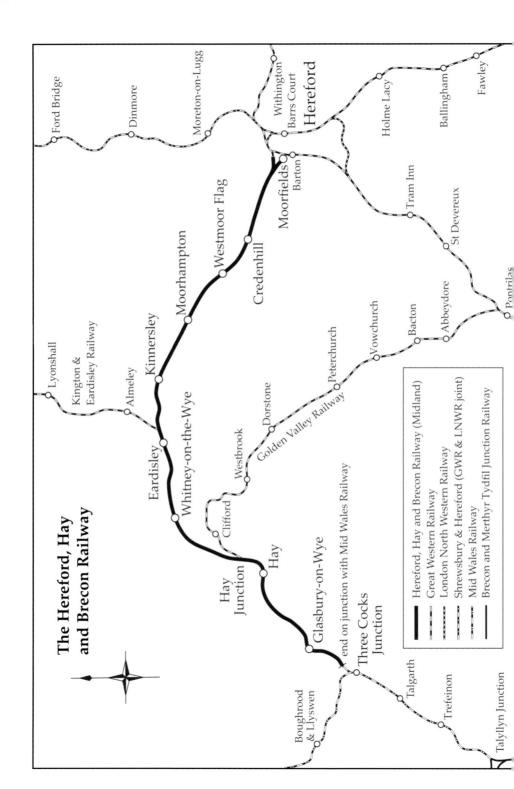

The Hereford, Hay
and Brecon Railway

Ford Bridge

Dinmore

Moreton-on-Lugg

Withington

Barrs Court

Hereford

Holme Lacy

Ballingham

Fawley

Moorfields

Barton

Tram Inn

Westmoor Flag

Credenhill

St Devereux

Moorhampton

Kinnersley

Almeley

Lyonshall

Kington &
Eardisley Railway

Pontrilas

Abbeydore

Bacton

Vowchurch

Peterchurch

Dorstone

Westbrook

Golden Valley Railway

Eardisley

Whitney-on-the-Wye

Clifford

Hay
Junction

Hay

Glasbury-on-Wye

end on junction with Mid Wales Railway

Three Cocks
Junction

Talgarth

Trefeinon

Boughrood
& Llyswen

Talyllyn Junction

Hereford, Hay and Brecon Railway (Midland)
Great Western Railway
London North Western Railway
Shrewsbury & Hereford (GWR & LNWR joint)
Mid Wales Railway
Brecon and Merthyr Tydfil Junction Railway

Preface

My recollections of my few journeys made over the Hereford, Hay and Brecon Railway – the HH&BR – are now necessarily distant. At that time I knew little about the origins and history of this apparently uncomplicated line extending from the city of Hereford to the county town of Brecknock. Later I learned that it had been built by three separate companies, and would experience many vicissitudes before it became part of the Midland Railway's corridor between the rich areas – mineral and maritime – of Swansea and the central counties of England. The halcyon days of the Hereford, Hay and Brecon Railway came in the first two decades of the 20th century, and after then the line gradually reverted to being the rural byway which it had been at the outset.

The stories of the other two companies – the Mid-Wales Railway and the Brecon and Merthyr Railway – responsible for two of the sections of the line to Brecon have already been told in other volumes in the Oakwood Library series. My hope has been to produce an account of the historical, operational and physical aspects of the remaining portion, extending from the western side of Hereford to meet the Mid-Wales Railway at a point just to the east of the idyllic Three Cocks Junction.

Over the years I have read as much as I could about this sequestered outpost of the Midland Railway and have gradually gathered information as it became available. For much of this I am deeply grateful to my friend and former colleague the late Colin Betts, to my pen-friend the late Jack Burrell, to the late Owen Humberstone Prosser, and to John Whiting of Welwyn Garden City, who was a fount of knowledge about the operation of the line. On signalling matters I am grateful to John Hinson, who runs the enlightening Signal Box website, and to his colleague Stuart Johnson, and to Reg Instone and Ian Wannell of the Signalling Record Society. I extend my thanks to the Lens of Sutton Association for providing illustrations of stations along the line, to John Alsop for the use of pictures from his collection and to Nicky Harden for allowing us to use pictures from her husband's, the late Tony Harden, collection. I also warmly thank the ever patient and helpful staff of the National Archives (formerly the Public Record Office). Lastly I wish to record my deep appreciation of the encouragement, patient advice and wise guidance which I have received from Lewis Hutton of Stenlake Publishing throughout the preparation of this book. In addition, Lewis's cartographic skills are seen in the clarity of the maps which he drew for pages 4, 6 and 14 below. To him and to his colleague Chris Potts, who commented upon the draft of the book, I offer my grateful thanks.

John Mair
Stanmore, Middlesex
April 2021

5

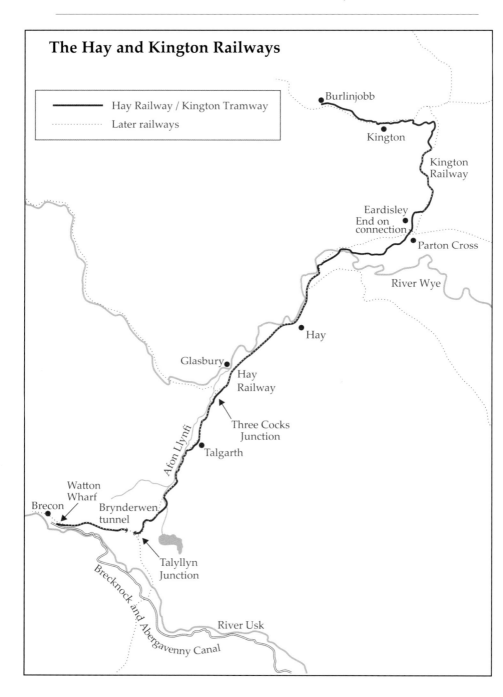

The Hay and Kington Railways

———	Hay Railway / Kington Tramway
·············	Later railways

Burlinjobb

Kington

Kington Railway

Eardisley
End on connection

Parton Cross

River Wye

Hay

Glasbury

Hay Railway

Three Cocks Junction

Talgarth

Afon Llynfi

Watton Wharf

Brecon

Brynderwen tunnel

Talyllyn Junction

Brecknock and Abergavenny Canal

River Usk

Chapter One

Historical Outline

West of Hereford a deep and reticent countryside extends to the Welsh Border. The landscape is one of great beauty, with arable lands and orchards spreading away from the meandering River Wye, northwards to the hilly country beyond which lie the River Arrow and Kington, and south-westwards to meet the steeps of the Black Mountains. On the far side of those mountains is found the valley of the River Usk, upon which stands the pleasant upland and county town of Brecon.

It is a quiet land, with sometimes a mystical feel about it. One learns without surprise that the poet Henry Vaughan was a native of Brecon; and that Thomas Traherne was once a Rector of Credenhill. Another local clergyman has become celebrated as a country diarist: Francis Kilvert.

The Hay and Kington Railways

The area seems an unlikely setting for early essays in railway building. But so it was: for in the year 1820 both the Hay and the Kington Railways were in operation. The Hay Railway Company was incorporated by an Act of 25th May, 1811, which authorized the construction of a railway, or tramroad, running from Watton Wharf on the Brecknock and Abergavenny Canal (which had opened on 24th December, 1800) at Brecon to run by way of Talgarth, Glasbury and Hay to Parton Cross, about one mile from the village of Eardisley in Herefordshire. A second Act, of 20th May, 1812, sanctioned a different and shorter route which included the building of a tunnel at Brynderwen, some four miles east of Brecon and a half-mile south of the village of Llanfihangel Tal-y-llyn, which was to give its name to the later Talyllyn Junction. The eastern terminus was also relocated to a point closer to Eardisley village. The line was built to a gauge of three feet six inches, and throughout its life was worked by horse traction. It was opened as far as Hay on 14th May, 1816, and was then progressively extended to Eardisley (24¼ miles from Brecon), reached on 1st December, 1818.

In the previous year, 1817, some of the leading citizens of Kington had resolved to promote a railway to connect the Hay Railway at Eardisley with their own town, and then to extend it westwards to the lime works at Burlinjobb (sometimes spelt Burlinjob or Burlingjobb), near Stanner. Construction of this line was authorized by the Kington Railway Act of

23rd May, 1818. The Kington Railway was also built to the gauge of three feet six inches, and was opened from an end-on junction with the Hay Railway at Eardisley (at a point north of the later Hereford, Hay and Brecon line station) to Kington on 1st May, 1820. The westward extension to Burlinjobb was delayed for some years, and was eventually completed in 1833.

The eastern end of the Brecknock and Abergavenny Canal was at Pontymoile (near Pontypool), where it joined the Monmouthshire Canal, which ran from Newport. The resultant link enabled the products of mines, quarries and ironworks to reach Brecon by water, and there to be transferred to the Hay and Kington Railways for the journey up-country to the Wye and Arrow Valleys, and in the reverse direction flowed some limestone, the output of an iron foundry in Kington, agricultural produce, and, possibly, woollen goods produced in Hay.

Although they provided a more reliable means of transport than the sometimes fitful River Wye, the two canals and the two railways offered a slow and circuitous route to their destinations. But a scheme proposed in the Railway Mania of the mid-1840s to build a main line from Worcester to West Wales, serving Herefordshire en route, attracted little firm support, and similarly another proposal to link Leominster with Hay and Brecon made no progress. A less ambitious scheme did, however, later materialize, and a line from a junction north of Leominster (on the Shrewsbury and Hereford Railway) to Kington was formally opened on 27th July, 1857.

In their own way, the horse-drawn trams of the Hay and Kington narrow gauge railways served their districts well for more than 40 years, and, although the traffic flows from and to Brecon were both uneven and unequal, the lines were, from a commercial point of view, quietly successful. During the 1850s, however, the inhabitants of Hay and Brecon began to desire a standard gauge railway which would connect with the by then rapidly developing national network.

Proposals for new railways

Sensible schemes put forward at various times to connect Brecon with Abergavenny by means of a railway following the valley of the River Usk failed to appeal sufficiently to investors and theorists alike, and were never implemented. In 1857, the Hon. Captain Walter Devereux of Tregoyd (near Glasbury) proposed the construction of a standard gauge railway to run from Hereford to Brecon via Hay. A relative of the Lord

Hereford who had been Chairman of the Hay Railway, and who had also favoured a new line following the Wye Valley from Hereford, Walter Devereux had a refreshingly realistic view of the possibilities. His hope was that the costs of a deliberately modest scheme could be contained, and that public spirit in western Herefordshire and in Brecknockshire could be enlisted in its support. Unfortunately, however, some local opinion favoured a more ambitious, and naturally more expensive, project by which a main line from Hereford would pass through the northern edge of Brecon and continue to the *El Dorado* of Swansea, of Milford Haven and of West Wales generally.

Discouraged by this lack of realism, Captain Devereux himself withdrew, but when, predictably, the trunk route scheme failed to secure financial credibility, his ideas for a Hereford, Hay and Brecon line began to bear fruit: local support now gathered strength and a Parliamentary Bill, to incorporate a company and to authorize construction of the railway, was prepared. In the summer of 1859 the promoters of the Hereford, Hay and Brecon Railway, as it became known (the HH&BR), entered negotiations with the proprietors of the Hay Railway with a view to buying their line and to utilizing at least some of its formation for the construction of the new standard gauge railway. Discussions were successful, and an agreement to purchase the Hay line was sealed in November 1859, by when the Hereford, Hay and Brecon Railway Act (*see below*) had been passed on 8th August, 1859.

This decision on the part of the Hereford line to buy the Hay Railway caused some disquiet in other quarters, for by now two other railway companies were aspiring to reach Brecon.

Incorporated by an Act of 1st August, 1859, the Brecon and Merthyr Tydfil Junction Railway (the B&MR) had been steadily forging northwards from Bassaleg Junction (near Newport). It went to the Rhymney Valley, and then, by means of reluctantly conceded running powers over a section of the Rhymney Railway, was to reach, by branch lines, the high industrial tablelands around Dowlais and the smoky amphitheatre of Merthyr Tydfil.

The B&MR main line continued northwards over the Brecon Beacons and then descended steeply to Talybont in the valley of the River Usk. The original, and natural, plan was to follow the Usk from Talybont to a terminus at Brecon, but, when – in the event never realized – plans for a railway from Abergavenny to Brecon via Talybont were put forward, the B&MR decided to give up the idea of building its own line into Brecon and instead to run its trains over the proposed new line from Abergavenny. Alas, the Usk Valley line never materialized, and the B&MR was left with an isolated and inconsequential outpost at Talybont. Nothing daunted, the B&MR decided to cross the Usk, to mount the Scethrog Ridge, and then to seek to follow the line of the Hay Railway from Brynderwen (Talyllyn) into Brecon.

The other contender for a route into Brecon, this time from the north, was the Mid-Wales Railway (MWR). Starting from Pentpontbren (1½ miles south of Llanidloes) this line ran southwards along the valleys of the Rivers Dulas, Marteg and Wye. The MWR Directors had set their sights, and their hearts, upon turning to the south-west near Builth Wells and then advancing to Llandovery. But in 1860 Parliament decided that Llandovery should be served by an extension of the already built Central Wales Railway, and the MWR realized, belatedly, that its future might lie with a route southward to the industrial areas and seaboard of Monmouthshire and Glamorganshire. In this, however, the MWR had been forestalled by the B&MR, who had by now developed a similar scheme, and the MWR could hope only for a line into Brecon. Coming south from Builth, it could join the course of the Hay Railway at Aberllynfi, south of Glasbury, and follow it as far as Brynderwen (Talyllyn), from where it would share the route of the B&MR for the final lap into Brecon. The station at Aberllynfi would become known as Three Cocks Junction, named after a local inn.

Both the B&MR and the MWR therefore had good cause to be alarmed by news of the proposed sale of the Hay Railway to the Hereford, Hay and Brecon Railway: they feared that the Hereford company would either treat the Three Cocks – Brynderwen (Talyllyn) – Brecon sections of the Hay Railway route as ransom strips and charge accordingly, or refuse access altogether. The MWR acquired some shares in the Hay company, but this step was not sufficient to block the sale to the HH&BR. As we shall see, there would, however, be in the event a reasonably satisfactory outcome.

In 1859 Parliament had a busy summer with Welsh and Welsh border railway schemes. On 1st August, a week before Royal Assent, given on 8th August, to the Hereford, Hay and Brecon Railway Act, Bills had been passed for the construction of the B&MR line from Dowlais to Talybont, and for that of the MWR line as far south as Newbridge, in the Wye valley above Builth. These were the enactments which set the scene for the concordat eventually reached between the parties for what would be, in effect, the partition of the Hay Railway.

The Hereford, Hay and Brecon Railway

We turn now to the Hereford, Hay and Brecon Railway Act itself. As well as incorporating the company, the Act of 8th August, 1859, dealt with financial matters. The authorized capital was £280,000, in £20 shares, and sanction was given to raise £93,000 in loans, the latter to be taken up only when all the shares had been subscribed, and when half of their value had been actually paid up. The number of Directors was fixed at seven, and the first Directors were individually named in the Act. It was stipulated that the company could not enter upon, take, or use any of the lands or property of the Hay Railway Company without the latter's written and sealed consent. The HH&BR was required to pay to the owner of the Whitney Toll Bridge (which spanned the River Wye) any amount by which the annual road bridge tolls should, after the opening of the railway, fall short of £345.

A private goods platform was to be constructed for the benefit of the occupiers of Trevithel Court Farm (near Pontithel) in the parish of Bronllys. A similar platform, with a crossing, was to be provided at Sheep House Farm, about 1½ miles south-west of Hay. The approval of the Admiralty was to be obtained for any crossings of the Wye where that river was tidal(!). Access to the land situated between the railway and the Wye at Hay was to be safeguarded. Powers of compulsory purchase were to lapse after three years, and construction of the railway was to be completed within five years from the passing of the Act.

Under the terms of the Act, the railway itself was to begin 'at or near the town of Brecon and in the parish of St John the Evangelist in the County of Brecon', and to terminate 'near Hereford in the parish of Holmer' by a junction with the Shrewsbury and Hereford Railway (S&HR) to the north-west of the city, and a short distance to the north of the (separate) junction (Barton Junction, later renamed Barrs Court Junction) where the lines to Barton station and to Barrs Court station diverged. (*This layout is described below.*) In reality, this proposed access arrangement would have been likely to give rise to delays, inconvenience, and even danger, as it would have been necessary for all trains arriving from the Brecon and Hay direction to reverse, or to be propelled southwards, from the junction with the S&HR if they were to reach either Barton or Barrs Court stations, and vice versa.

Subsequently, different arrangements were proposed at the Hereford end of the line, and these were authorized by the Hereford, Hay and Brecon Railway (Deviation) Act of 3rd July, 1860. Instead of joining the Shrewsbury and Hereford at the point envisaged in the 1859 Act, the

HH&BR line was now to turn southwards and to form a junction with the Newport, Abergavenny and Hereford line near Barton, on the west side of the city. (On 1st July, 1860, just before Royal Assent was given to the Deviation Act, the Newport, Abergavenny and Hereford Railway had become part of the new West Midland Railway.) Although more rational, and theoretically much more convenient, these revised junction arrangements were to be a source – to be described below – of tribulation for the HH&BR.

On 15th May, 1860, the B&MR had obtained Parliamentary powers to extend its line from Talybont to Brynderwen (Talyllyn) and to Brecon in the manner described above, while on 3rd July in the same year the MWR was authorized to build its line from Newbridge to Three Cocks and to Brynderwen (Talyllyn), and from there to have running powers over the B&MR line into Brecon.

The way now lay open for negotiations between the HH&BR and the Brecon & Merthyr and the Mid-Wales Railways over the future use of the route of the Hay Railway, and, as we have seen, the resultant agreement was that the B&MR would take over the section between Brecon and Brynderwen (Talyllyn), the Mid-Wales would take the section between Talyllyn and a point (just to the east of the future Three Cocks Junction) near Glasbury-on-Wye, from where the final section to Eardisley would be taken by the HH&BR.

On 6th August, 1860, the Hay Railway Act was passed, giving effect to the agreements described above. Vesting took place on 22nd August, 1860 (and the Hay Railway Company was finally wound up in 1862). The HH&BR was now at liberty to use the Hay Railway alignment between Eardisley and a point 29 chains east of Three Cocks Junction. From this point the MWR planned to build an east to west chord connecting the Hereford line with its own line north of Three Cocks: this link would complete a triangular junction (comparable with that at Talyllyn), which would enable southbound MWR trains to run directly onto the line to Hereford, and vice versa. Some preliminary earthworks for this chord were carried out, but the connecting line was never built. The section between the proposed end-on junction on the Hereford line and Three Cocks was, however, to become and to remain the property of the MWR; and at Three Cocks Junction the buildings and signal box were of typical MWR design, being quite different from that of the stations and signal boxes along the Hereford line.

The Mid-Wales Railway was to buy the portion starting from the junction with the HH&BR (*above*), and ending at a junction with the Brecon and Merthyr Railway at what became Talyllyn Junction, whilst the B&MR would take over the Hay Railway route between Talyllyn Junction and Brecon. Thus, notwithstanding its title, the HH&BR would actually own only the line between the western edge of Hereford and a point east of Three Cocks Junction. The division of the Hay Railway route in this way was probably to the liking of the HH&BR and of the MWR, as it left the B&MR to carry out the difficult, and no doubt costly, enlargement of the tunnel west of Talyllyn Junction to accommodate the standard gauge trains of all three companies! Again, Parliamentary sanction was required to legitimize the final arrangements: the MWR received theirs on 12th June, 1861, and the B&MR theirs on 6th August, 1861.

Some further legislation was to follow. Two further HH&BR Acts made mainly detailed changes, although the Act of 1859 remained the principal measure. The Hereford, Hay and Brecon Railway Act of 30th June, 1862 authorized certain variations from the originally approved line and levels between Three Cocks and Whitney, and made some consequential alterations, such as the resiting of the Sheep House Farm platform required by the principal Act. (In fact this platform was never built.) The Hereford, Hay and Brecon Railway Act of 4th May, 1863 authorized an increase of up to £75,000 in the share capital and an increase of up to £25,000 in the borrowing powers.

Access to Hereford

At this point a digression may be made to trace the terminal arrangements of the various railways which entered, or sought to enter, Hereford. For many years, the provision of satisfactory accommodation for railway passengers in Hereford presented intractable problems, and indeed there was no ready or clear-cut solution. The overriding constraint was that the historic core of the city was of a layout, nature and importance which precluded the building of a single, central, station, and it followed that any station (or stations) would need to be built on the margins of what was then a compact country town.

The problem was exacerbated by the general British aversion to any form of central *dirigisme*, and by the fact that no fewer than five separate railway companies desiring to enter Hereford all had their own needs and preferences, in pursuance of which they were prepared to be as fully uncooperative, and indeed as obstructive, as they considered to be necessary. The result was a series of impasses which lasted for many

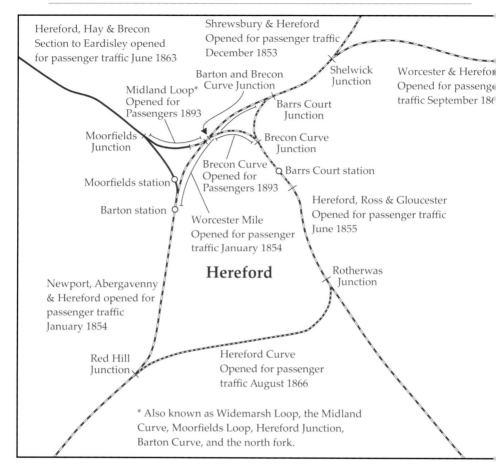

Hereford, Hay & Brecon Section to Eardisley opened for passenger traffic June 1863

Shrewsbury & Hereford Opened for passenger traffic December 1853

Barton and Brecon Curve Junction

Midland Loop* Opened for Passengers 1893

Shelwick Junction

Worcester & Herefor Opened for passeng traffic September 186

Barrs Court Junction

Moorfields Junction

Brecon Curve Junction

Moorfields station

Brecon Curve Opened for Passengers 1893

Barrs Court station

Barton station

Worcester Mile Opened for passenger traffic January 1854

Hereford, Ross & Gloucester Opened for passenger traffic June 1855

Newport, Abergavenny & Hereford opened for passenger traffic January 1854

Hereford

Rotherwas Junction

Red Hill Junction

Hereford Curve Opened for passenger traffic August 1866

* Also known as Widemarsh Loop, the Midland Curve, Moorfields Loop, Hereford Junction, Barton Curve, and the north fork.

years, and which gave rise to continual inconvenience for the travelling public. The numerous difficulties and delays which thus arose are narrated in meticulous detail by Gordon Wood in his book *Railways of Hereford*, published by the author in conjunction with the Kidderminster Railway Museum in 2003. From our point of view, the salient points, in chronological order, would appear to be as follows.

In July 1852 the Shrewsbury and Hereford Railway (which had been incorporated in August 1846) began running goods trains to Hereford, and, on 6th December, 1853, commenced passenger services to a temporary (and apparently desolate) terminus situated to the south of the site of the future and permanent Barrs Court station on the *east* side of the city: construction of this station began in 1854, and proceeded rapidly.

On 16th January, 1854, and coming north, the Newport, Abergavenny and Hereford Railway (NA&HR) opened its line, again to a temporary terminus, this time located to the south of the future Barton station on the *west* side of the city. It was envisaged that the new, permanent, station would be a terminus, and to this end the architect James Clayton designed a large, well proportioned and impressive building in the Italian Renaissance style. In 1853, however, it was decided that the Worcester and Hereford Railway, approaching the city from the north over a section of the Shrewsbury and Hereford (joined at Shelwick Junction, 76 chains north-east of the Barton, later Barrs Court, Junction, described below), would also use Barton, which would thus become a through rather than a terminal station; and accordingly James Clayton produced a much modified design for the station in order to meet the changed requirements.

Although, in the event, the Worcester and Hereford Railway would not be completed throughout until 1861, the line through Barton was in 1854 extended northwards for a distance of one mile and 7 chains to meet the Shrewsbury and Hereford Railway at a point at first called Barton Junction but later, and permanently, renamed Barrs Court Junction.

This new connection became known as 'the Worcester Mile', and was of great importance. Traffic – and particularly coal traffic from the Eastern and Western Valleys of Monmouthshire – could now proceed directly from South Wales to Shrewsbury and beyond to Chester and to Birkenhead. Coming south, passenger and goods trains from the Shrewsbury and Worcester lines could run either over the Worcester Mile to Barton, or directly to Barrs Court; and, from our point of view, the use of short sections of the Worcester Mile would enable trains to and from the line to Hay and Brecon to reach, at various times, both Barton and Barrs Court stations.

The broad gauge (7 feet and 0¼ inches wide) Hereford, Ross and Gloucester Railway (HR&GR) opened its line from Grange Court Junction (7½ miles south of Gloucester, and situated on the (also broad gauge) South Wales Railway) to Hereford early in June 1855, and ran its trains to the as yet incomplete Barrs Court station, where the firm of Eassie of Gloucester had erected a temporary building (this company, as we shall see, would provide many of the station buildings along the line of the HH&BR). Largely completed in 1856, the permanent Barrs Court station building, designed by John Penson in a blend of Gothic and Tudor styles, was, and remains to this day, an impressive building. The 'Barrs Court' after which it was named was a substantial house in the vicinity, the home of the De la Barre family. It was subsequently converted to a (currently special) school.

Barrs Court station was something of a frontier point, for the broad gauge line coming from Gloucester and Ross terminated facing the end – across an intermediate concourse – of the standard gauge Shrewsbury and Hereford line coming from the north. A loop line of mixed (i.e. dual) gauge track behind the main station connected the two systems. This state of affairs persisted until August 1869, when the HR&GR was converted from broad to standard gauge, and a more extensive and flexible track layout at Barrs Court became possible. The central concourse (situated between the respective ends of the S&HR and the HR&GR) was removed, as were some other structures, and the land thus cleared was used to create an entirely new island platform, between which and the original main platform four tracks were laid, two adjacent to platform faces, and two central through lines. A further line was added on the east side of the new island platform, upon which stood a long, canopied, building, and which was connected to the main platform by means of a covered footbridge.

On 1st July, 1860, the West Midland Railway was formed by an amalgamation of the Oxford, Worcester and Wolverhampton Railway and of the Newport, Abergavenny and Hereford Railway. These two systems were physically separate, but they were to be bridged by the Worcester and Hereford Railway which was finally opened in 1861, and which too formed part of the new West Midland Railway – new, but short-lived, since in 1861 it was leased to the Great Western Railway (GWR), and two years later, on 1st August, 1863, amalgamated with that company. The absorption of these lines by the GWR was to have repercussions for the Midland Railway, and in particular for the latter's tenure of the HH&BR.

Another, and perhaps key, element in the maze of Hereford railways was the Brecon Curve. This was intended to be a direct connection between the Worcester Mile and Barrs Court station, and it was to enable trains moving north from Barton to reach Barrs Court directly, without travelling to, and then reversing at, Barrs Court Junction (which had initially been called Barton Junction).

The Brecon Curve had a sufficiently astonishing history. Its construction was authorized by the Great Western Railway (Additional Powers) Act of 1865, and work – which included a bridge over the Herefordshire and Gloucestershire Canal and a level crossing at the Burcott Road – began in 1866. Construction proceeded quickly, but was abruptly halted in November of that year, when it became clear that the HH&BR – for whose benefit the Curve was primarily being provided – might not be in a position to take advantage of it. There the matter rested, until it was realized that the statutory powers to construct it would expire in 1870. Hence, in the early part of that year, work was hastily resumed, and a connection was made with the Shrewsbury and Hereford line 30 chains to the north of Barrs Court station, but no connection was laid with the Worcester Mile. A token train was run over the new length of line, whereupon the GWR lifted some rails at the eastern end of the Curve, thereby making it incapable of further use.

For more than 20 years no material changes took place. Eventually an agreement was reached between the Midland Railway and the London and North Western Railway (LNWR) and GWR companies for HH&BR line trains to run over a new connection (the Moorfields Loop, to be discussed below, page 33) to join the Worcester Mile, and then to traverse the Brecon Curve in order to reach Barrs Court station, where, after much vacillation and many changes of plan, the LNWR and GWR had finally agreed that passenger traffic should be concentrated. Early in 1892 work began upon restoring and upgrading the Curve, and at last, on 2nd January, 1893, more than 27 years after the enabling Act had been passed, HH&BR passenger trains began to run to and from Barrs Court over the Brecon Curve.

Finally, and to complete this summary, mention must be made of the construction by the London and North Western Railway of a loop line which enabled traffic from the Newport and Abergavenny direction to reach Barrs Court without travelling via Barton and without reversal at Barrs Court Junction. (The LNWR enjoyed running powers over the NA&HR route, and indeed had worked this line for the first year after it had opened in 1854.) The avoiding line, 2 miles and 10 chains in length and known as 'the Hereford Curve', ran well to the south of the city. It began at Redhill Junction, near the village of Grafton, on the NA&HR and ran eastwards, and then northwards, to join the HR&G line at Rotherwas Junction, 1 mile and 15 chains south of the (permanent) Barrs Court station. Between Rotherwas and Barrs Court the GWR laid mixed gauge track, which lasted until 1869, when, as noted above, the Hereford and Gloucester was converted to standard gauge. The new loop was opened on 16th July, 1866, and had of course the effect of abstracting some traffic from the NA&HR line through Barton. The latter did, however, retain much importance both as an interchange point and as a destination, especially for goods and livestock traffic destined for the city; and until 1893 it remained a significant place for the HH&BR. Today the Hereford Curve forms the one and only means of railway access from the south to the city.

Construction of the Hereford, Hay and Brecon Railway

Construction of the whole line between Hereford and Brecon had begun with the turning of the first sod by Lady Tredegar at Penlan Farm, near Brecon, on 10th April, 1860. The works had been entrusted to the contractors McCormick and Holme, who initially made good progress but who then withdrew after being offended by the substitution of a local man for the HH&BR Director who had been instrumental in their appointment. So far as the HH&BR was concerned, these contractors were replaced by the redoubtable Thomas Savin, the energetic and usually highly effective builder and entrepreneur who was responsible for much railway and other construction in Wales. He went about the task with his usual enthusiasm, and, at his own expense, built a new bridge to replace an old one over the River Wye at Hay, a project over which the HH&BR Directors had been hesitating.

As already stated, the general course of the Hay Railway was followed in the construction of the three sections between Brecon and Eardisley. The replacement of what was essentially a horse-powered tramway with a standard gauge railway worked by steam locomotives did, however, inevitably require many adjustments, particularly in matters of levels and of curvature. There were some major departures

Westbound train at the down platform of Hay station, probably headed by MR 0-4-4T locomotive. The leading coach is probably a through carriage from Birmingham. In the background is the bridge built by Thomas Savin over the River Wye. It was replaced in 1958 by a concrete bridge. *John Alsop collection*

from the Hay route at, for example, Trefeinon and south and north of Talgarth on the MWR section, and both west and east of Whitney on the HH&BR's own section. There were numerous minor deviations, and it has been calculated that of the approximately 24¼ miles of the formation (as distinct from the route) of the Hay Railway only about 9 were actually used for the new line of railway: 2¼ miles in the B&MR section between Brecon and Talyllyn (including the tunnel); 3¾ miles in the MWR section between Talyllyn and Three Cocks; and 3 miles in the HH&BR section between Three Cocks and Eardisley. Nevertheless, the following of the general route and course of the Hay Railway greatly facilitated the construction of the Brecon to Hereford line as a whole and led to substantial cost savings.

Although construction, particularly at the Hereford end of the line, was at first hampered by the slowness of landowners in finalizing the sales to the HH&BR of the areas required for the railway, all the land acquisitions were in the event completed without any recourse to compulsory purchase powers. Further west, the piling for the river bridge to the west of Whitney took longer than expected, but this too was accomplished without excessive delay.

The most arduous task in the construction of the line was the formation of the Norton Canon cutting, situated to the west of Moorhampton station. Through it, westbound trains descended at a gradient of 1 in 60 towards Kinnersley. At its deepest point, the floor of the cutting was 35 feet below ground level, and altogether the removal of some 150,000 cubic yards of soil was necessary. This soil consisted mainly of clay and sand, and in wet weather became a morass which was extremely difficult to work. It was much to the credit of the contractors and of their workforce that, when finished, the cutting presented an exceptionally neat appearance. Although less severe, difficulties were also encountered in forming two cuttings near Clifford, in the section between Whitney and Hay.

In general, the standard of construction of the line between Hereford and the junction with the Mid-Wales Railway 29 chains east of Three Cocks Junction was very satisfactory, and only quite minor improvements or alterations were specified when the Government Inspectors visited the railway.

The approval of the Board of Trade for the opening of the line for passenger traffic was obtained in stages. In June, 1863, Captain Rich of the Railway Inspectorate approved, for the passage of passenger trains, the section between Hereford (Moorfields) and Eardisley; shortly before 11th July, 1864, the section between Eardisley and Hay was

cleared for passenger traffic; in September, 1864, Captain Tyler passed
the section between Hay and the end-on junction with the MWR 29
chains east of Three Cocks Junction; and in the following month,
October, 1864, Colonel Yolland passed the 'last lap' between that end-
on junction and Three Cocks Junction itself.

The smooth ride experienced by passengers was locally praised, and
was attributed to the quality and to the depth of the ballast, obtained
from the pit situated at Stretton Sugwas. The bridges, many of which
were built from locally quarried stone, were also commended for their
design, workmanship and finished appearance.

The line was single throughout, with passing loops at some of the
stations. It was, however, envisaged that the line would eventually be
doubled, and provision was made accordingly at the various overline
and underline bridges. Expense was incurred in building some of the
overline bridges where level crossings might have been installed, but
over time the additional monies thus spent were probably more than
recovered by savings in running costs and by gains in convenience.

Gradients

From Hereford the line followed, generally, the northern side of the
valley of the River Wye before turning south to cross the river itself west
of Whitney, and then continuing on its southern side to Hay and to
Glasbury. Hence, whilst quite frequently changing to follow the lie of
the land, the gradients were in the main mostly unremarkable and
seldom steep. Exceptions were that, as it ascended to the summit (364
feet 8 inches) just to the east of Moorhampton station, the line rose for
more than a mile (past Westmoor Flag station) at a gradient of 1 in 120,
and then fell for a short distance at 1 in 99 to the station, beyond which
there was a further short fall at 1 in 170 and then, for more than a mile,
a longer descent at 1 in 60. This relatively steep incline could present a
problem to up trains, and, as we shall see, it was sometimes necessary
for up goods trains to be double headed, or to be divided at Kinnersley,
so that they could be brought uphill in two portions.

To the west of Eardisley there were short rises at 1 in 102, 161 and 120,
before the line descended at 1 in 334 and 147 to Whitney and to the river
crossing. Between Hay and Glasbury there were some short upward
pitches at 1 in 84 and 80; and between the end-on junction with the Mid-
Wales and Three Cocks Junction station there was a brief ascent at 1 in
75, followed by another rise, this time at 1 in 264, into the station.

Train services begin

The HH&BR line was opened in stages from the eastern end. In Hereford the trains ran from a temporary terminus at Moorfields, a short distance north-west of the junction at Barton with the Newport, Abergavenny and Hereford Railway, which, as we have seen, had, on 1st July, 1860, become part of the West Midland Railway (WMR), a concern which was in turn 'amalgamated' with (in practice, virtually absorbed by) the Great Western Railway in 1863. The Moorfields temporary terminus, which was situated on the south-west side of the railway, was of a very simple character, and consisted of a single platform reached by a narrow unmade lane. This interim arrangement arose from the fact the Board of Trade (which had a generally supervisory role in relation to railways) was not satisfied that the junction which then existed between the HH&BR and the Worcester Mile, and which thus gave access to Barton station, was adequate for regular passenger traffic. This junction was later modified, and signalled, to make it suitable for passenger trains to run to and from Barton as from 1st October, 1864. Theoretically, these changes made it possible for HH&BR passenger trains to gain access to Barton station and to close the platform at Moorfields, but, as we shall see, the latter is not what happened until some years later.

On 24th October, 1862, the line was opened from Hereford to Moorhampton for the conveyance of coal and lime; and on 30th June, 1863, both passenger and goods trains began to run as far as Eardisley. Services were extended to Hay on 11th July, 1864.

The B&MR officially opened its line to Brecon on 1st May, 1863 (although some trains had been running since 23rd April of that year), but HH&BR services to that town had of course to await the completion of the intermediate MWR portion between Three Cocks and Talyllyn. A ceremonial train from Brecon to Llanidloes and back was run on 23rd August, 1864, and the Three Cocks to Talyllyn section was opened to mineral traffic on 1st September, 1864. On Monday 19th September, 1864, HH&BR passenger and goods trains began to run, via the MWR and B&MR sections, through to Brecon. MWR passenger services to Brecon began two days later, on 21st September. All three companies used the B&MR's simple terminus at Watton, not far from the end of the Brecknock and Abergavenny Canal which lay at the beginning of our story.

The HH&BR company owned no locomotives, and probably no rolling stock, and when train services began in 1862 they were at first provided by the WMR, and then, from 1863, by the WMR's successor, the Great Western Railway. When, in 1864, it became possible to introduce through services to Brecon, it was Thomas Savin who, as contractor both to the HH&BR and to the B&MR, took over the responsibility of running the trains between Hereford and Brecon.

Amalgamation with the Brecon and Merthyr ...

The relationship between the Hereford, Hay and Brecon Railway and the Brecon and Merthyr Railway thus became close, and it seemed a natural progression to amalgamate the two railways, although, as is often the case with mergers, one party, in this instance the B&MR, was predominant. In accordance with the Brecon and Merthyr (Amalgamation) Act of 5th July, 1865, Parliament authorized the B&MR to take over the HH&BR, and an agreement made on 2nd August, 1865, between the two companies for the transfer of the HH&BR to the B&MR took effect on 25th August in the same year, from when the B&MR managed and operated, and received the income from, the combined railways. Two major misfortunes were, however, in store.

The year 1866 was one of severe economic depression, and the financial commitments arising from Thomas Savin's manifold activities and interests overwhelmed him. His ensuing failure resulted in personal bankruptcy, and the enlarged B&MR lost its guiding hand. The company was unable to pay the interest on its debentures and on its loan stock, and it was accordingly placed in the hands of a Receiver.

Then it emerged that the agreement of 2nd August, 1865 (*above*) had not been ratified by the B&MR preference shareholders. The matter was laid before the Court of Chancery, who held that because of the procedural flaw the amalgamation was null and void and of no effect.

... and Separation

The invalidity of the amalgamation was recognized and corrected by a further Act of Parliament, namely the Brecon and Merthyr Railway Arrangement Act of 13th July, 1868. The HH&BR now resumed its separate existence, but had insufficient funds with which to meet its financial obligations. Hence it too passed into the hands of the Receiver. A further measure, the Hereford, Hay and Brecon Railway Act of 26th July, 1869, reconstituted the company and provided for a capital reconstruction, as a result of which it was able to become independent once more.

After this parting of the ways in 1868 between the B&MR and the HH&BR, the MWR was prevailed upon to provide the train service between Hereford and Brecon. Somewhat reluctantly, it agreed to do so for one year, from 1st October, 1868 until 30th September, 1869. One positive step which it took was to resume running passenger trains into Barton station: in order to save money the B&MR had on 1st July, 1867 suspended that arrangement and terminated its trains at the bleak Moorfields.

Enter the Midland Railway

The tentacular Midland Railway by no means confined itself to the Midland counties of England. By its own and by connecting lines, its operations were to extend to Bournemouth and to Southampton in the south, to Great Yarmouth and to Lowestoft in the east, and to Glasgow and to Edinburgh in the north. In the 1860s the Midland aspired to reach the immense mineral and maritime riches of South and West Wales. A particular objective was Swansea Bay, with its well situated port of Swansea itself and with the resources – such as high grade anthracite and copper – of the hinterland. Of particular importance was the highly productive industry of copper smelting, which drew its raw material of copper both from indigenous sources and from all over the world; and this process was aided by the availability of local and top quality coal needed for smelting. The Midland discerned that a series of independent lines could, in the aggregate, provide a through route from Swansea and Llanelly to the heartlands of England.

The MR had obtained running powers over the GWR line from Worcester to Hereford, and, upon learning that the MWR had agreed to operate the service between Hereford to Brecon for only one year, offered to operate that line on and from 1st October, 1869. One may imagine with what relief and pleasure the HH&BR directors listened to this proposal. The solid, dependable, Midland would take over the practicalities of running the trains, whilst the HH&BR company would receive a reliable income.

Accordingly, under the terms of an agreement dated 2nd August, 1869, the HH&BR granted to the MR exclusive running rights over its lines. Almost immediately, however, a difficulty arose. Sensing, correctly, that both the B&MR and the MWR would, sooner or later, fall into its hands, the GWR had been content for both companies to run HH&B trains into Barton station, and, pending eventual takeover, could reap the benefit of collecting some welcome access charges for entry to, and occupation of, what was by now an underused station, for by this stage most of Hereford's passenger trains were running to and from Barrs Court.

In the event, the impecunious B&MR wished to avert these access charges (of £620 annually), and, in order to obviate the use of Barton, had in 1867 re-established the temporary and rudimentary platform at Moorfields on the south curve leading to Barton station itself. From 30th June, 1867, the B&MR no longer ran its trains into Barton, but terminated them at Moorfields. This move may have been unwise, since this bleak Moorfields station was reached by a still unmade and muddy track and, devoid of any amenities, was hardly an inducement for prospective passengers to use the trains. The MWR, which took over the operation on 1st October, 1868, was not wealthy, but it was more accommodating and did, sensibly, run its trains all the way into Barton. For this privilege a reduced annual charge of £450 was made.

When, however, the Midland Railway arranged to assume operation of the railway route to Hay and Brecon, the GWR apprehended that the MR had designs upon the lucrative South Wales traffic, and took a very different line from that which it had adopted towards the B&MR and the MWR. It now forbade HH&BR trains to enter Barton station, and maintained that the use of the station was not transferable when the Midland took over the HH&BR operation on and from 1st October, 1869.

Access by the Midland to Barton was therefore refused, and this prohibition took the tangible form of placing an engine and coal wagons on the connecting south curve. Mr S. E. Bolden, Chairman of the HH&BR, sent a letter of protest to Sir Daniel Gooch, Chairman of the GWR, but, predictably, this was to no avail, and the MR was obliged to revert to the use of a (slightly altered) temporary station on the HH&BR land at Moorfields, to which public access remained withal both awkward and inconvenient. To the reconstituted station the MR added a simple, and apparently comfortless, waiting shed.

Legal proceedings ensued, and, after various reversals, it seemed in 1870 that the GWR had prevailed. The effect of the GWR decision and actions was thus to isolate the HH&BR and to make it impossible for MR trains – whether passenger or goods – from Worcester (and beyond) to proceed to the Brecon line. This state of affairs was to persist for some three years.

Matters came to a head, however, when, after all of its attempts to persuade the GWR to change its mind had been unsuccessful, the MR attempted on 18th April, 1871, to run a train over the curve between Moorfields and Barton. The GWR again responded by blocking the line with an engine and wagons. A loyal Midland driver, in charge of a larger engine, was anxious to move the offending GWR train out of the way. Discretion prevailed, however, and the Midland tried further litigation instead.

The case was eventually heard in the Rolls Court early in 1873. In February of that year, Lord Romilly, the Master of the Rolls, found for the defendants, the GWR, and he held that, although the HH&BR itself had a legal right to run to Barton, the local company was not entitled to delegate that right to another party (in this case the Midland Railway). It followed that the MR had no right to use the junction north of Barton or to enter Barton station. He dismissed the MR's suit, and made an award of costs against the Midland.

Lord Romilly's decision was, however, reversed when the undaunted Midland made an appeal, which was heard in April 1873. The Lords Justices ruled that there was nothing in the agreement between the HH&BR and the MR which was illegal or contrary to public policy, and that the appellants were entitled to use Barton. This time it was the turn of the GWR to meet the costs.

After the appeal decision, the way lay open for the Midland to operate through trains from its own system onto the HH&BR line, and this it began to do on 8th July, 1873, when it started to run through carriages from Birmingham (New Street) to Brecon, by way of Stoke Works Junction, Droitwich, Worcester and Hereford. It was of course also possible to run through goods trains. On 1st April, 1874, the MR began to use the station at Barton as well as the curve, and the by now redundant and temporary station at Moorfields could at last be closed. The interval between the appeal decision, in April, 1873, in favour of the Midland and the commencement, nearly one year later, of the MR's use of Barton is perhaps to be explained by the wish of the Midland to be assured that its desired lease of the HH&BR would take effect: this it did at the beginning of July 1874, the month during which Parliamentary approval was forthcoming. The through carriage service between Birmingham and Brecon (and later, from 2nd July, 1877, Swansea) continued for many years, until it was withdrawn, as a wartime economy measure, on 31st December, 1916. It was never restored.

Swansea Vale; and Neath and Brecon

On 1st September, 1874, the MR acquired the Swansea Vale Railway (SVR), which ran from Swansea to Brynamman, via Ystalyfera. Another concern, the Swansea Vale and Neath and Brecon Junction Railway (SV and N&BJR), had been authorized on 29th July, 1864, to build a connecting line, 7 miles and 22 chains in length, from a junction at Ynisygeinon, just south of Ystalyfera on the SVR, to Colbren Junction on the Neath and Brecon Railway (N&BR). This SV and N&BJR was to have been leased to the N&BR, but was in the event amalgamated with that company by the Neath and Brecon Railway (Amalgamation and Arrangement) Act of 26th July, 1869. Mutual running powers over their respective systems had been agreed between the SVR and the N&BR, and so when the Midland acquired the SVR in 1874 it also gained running powers over the N&BR, to the initial chagrin of the latter. Using the connecting line between Colbren and Ynisygeinon Junctions, the Midland could thus run through from Brecon to Ynisygeinon (a distance of 29 miles), and thereby obtained complete liberty to reach Swansea from any part of its system. Through carriages between Birmingham (New Street) and the Swansea Vale station (St Thomas) in Swansea were introduced on Monday 2nd July, 1877.

The Midland also agreed to provide most services over the N&BR, leaving the N&BR itself to operate only the service between Neath and Colbren (and, from 1900, a few goods trains over the Colbren to Brecon section). With one short interval in 1889 when the N&BR briefly took direct action in an attempt to alter the terms of its contract, these arrangements continued peaceably until 1922, when (by means of the

Eardisley station looking west, a Great Western train stands at the up platform. 1909.
Tony Harden collection

Great Western Railway (Western Group) Preliminary Absorption Scheme (No. 2) of 24th July, 1922) the N&BR became part of the GWR just in advance of the Grouping; this was one of a number of amalgamations which took place before the main Grouping itself took effect on 1st January, 1923. Even then the London Midland and Scottish Railway (LMS), as successor to the MR, continued to provide the services for some years, until Hereford to Swansea through services finally ceased on 31st December, 1930. Thereafter – and at last! – the GWR assumed complete responsibility for operating the Neath and Brecon lines.

Leasing and purchase of the HH&BR

Meanwhile, the Midland Railway (Hereford, Hay and Brecon Railway Lease) Act (July, 1874), had empowered the MR to convert its exclusive running powers over the HH&B into a lease of the railway. Just over a decade later, the Midland Railway (Additional Powers) Act of 16th July, 1885, enabled the MR to purchase the HH&BR, and vesting took place in the following year, 1886. After a not altogether happy career of some 27 years, the HH&BR company was dissolved.

The Kington and Eardisley Railway

Meanwhile, a further development (unrelated to the above) had taken place on 3rd August, 1874, when a new line, 6 miles and 72 chains in length, was opened between Titley Junction (1¾ miles east of Kington) and Eardisley Junction. This new line, the Kington and Eardisley Railway (K&ER), had been authorized some years previously (on 30th June, 1862), and, just as the HH&BR had followed parts of the course of the Hay Railway, so did the K&ER, where practicable, replace parts of the three feet six inches gauge Kington Railway. The new line left the Leominster and Kington line immediately east of Titley Junction, and ran southwards, climbing to a summit just south of Lyonshall (or Lyons Hall) station. It then descended steeply through Almeley, where there was also a station, to the Wye Valley and joined the HH&BR at a junction 5 chains east of Eardisley station.

The K&ER was a simple but relatively expensive line to build. Unfortunately it knew little prosperity. In 1897 it was cheaply acquired by the GWR, who closed it on 1st January, 1917, the lightly worn rails apparently being considered of more value to the war effort than to the rural economy. In the face of local pressures, the GWR somewhat reluctantly relaid the line and restored services in 1922 (from Titley to Almeley on 18th September and then from Almeley to Eardisley on 11th December, 1922). But the line was for a second time closed, on 1st July, 1940, again ostensibly as a wartime economy, and this time it did not reopen. A short length of the line at the Eardisley end was, however, retained in order to provide access to a fuel depot, and to store spare rolling stock.

The Golden Valley Railway

The HH&BR received another connection when in 1889 it was joined at Hay Junction, 23 chains north of Hay station, by the Golden Valley Railway (GVR). This was an independent line, which began at Pontrilas, situated on the line between Hereford and Abergavenny, and ran north-westwards along the beautiful valley of the River Dore to Dorstone. From here an extension was built to Hay Junction, along which goods traffic began to run on 21st April, 1889, and passenger trains on 27th May in the same year. The 23 chains were doubled beween Hay station and Hay Junction, where a signal box, of Midland Railway design, was provided, largely at the expense of the GVR.

Although the GVR Directors had highly ambitious plans for their railway (they envisaged an eastward extension to Monmouth and to the Bristol Channel), the reality was that, running through beautiful but sparsely populated countryside, their line was unremunerative, and, scarcely nine years after passenger trains began to run to Hay, the whole line was closed, on 20th April, 1898. In accordance with its usual practice upon seeing a local line in difficulty, the GWR bought it for the proverbial song – in this case for £11,000, about one-thirtieth of the costs of construction. The GWR then overhauled and upgraded the GVR, and reopened the line in its entirety on 1st May, 1901. Passenger services then ran for some 40 years until they were withdrawn (as yet another alleged wartime economy) on 15th December, 1941, although goods trains continued until the Hay extension from Dorstone was closed completely on 2nd January, 1950 (there being no Sunday service, the last goods train ran on Saturday 31st December, 1949). After this truncation, the track north of Dorstone was recovered by engineering teams, the layout at Hay Junction was simplified, and the signal box at Hay Junction was abolished by April 1950.

The absentee London and North Western Railway

At this point it may be asked why the London and North Western Railway did not make a bid to obtain running powers over, or indeed to take over, the Hereford, Hay and Brecon line, for the larger company (which was to become the largest joint stock company in the world) was always vigilant for opportunities to expand its system. The conjectural answer would appear to be threefold.

Firstly, the LNWR could reach South Wales by a variety of routes, which with the passage of time grew in number. First, and coming south, access to Newport lay via the Newport, Abergavenny and Hereford Railway, running powers over which also conferred the benefit of the use of the Taff Vale Extension line, which, running broadly westwards from Pontypool Road, took trains transversely across the Valleys to Quakers Yard and thence to Middle Duffryn (between Mountain Ash and Aberdare), where they met, at an end-on junction, the mixed gauge Vale of Neath Railway. In turn the Vale of Neath Railway both provided a line into Neath itself and also led to the mineral and maritime riches of Swansea and of its district. (Possibly a little confusingly, the term 'The Vale of Neath Railway' came to be applied to the entire, combined, line between Neath and Pontypool Road, but it more strictly belongs to the section between Neath and Middle Duffryn, and to a branch leading from Gelli Tarw junction (above Aberdare) to Merthyr Tydfil.)

Second, the LNWR had a relationship, sometimes turbulent, with the Merthyr, Tredegar and Abergavenny Railway (MT&AR), and with the series of railways which led, from the numerous junctions along the MT&AR route, to Newport, to Cardiff and to South Wales generally. These railways ran down the valleys of the Ebbw Fach, the Ebbw Fawr, the Sirhowy, the Rhymney and the Taff rivers. It was of course also possible to use these valley lines to convey goods northwards as well as southwards, and so to bring coal and other minerals to the MT&AR junctions for onward transmission to Abergavenny and to Hereford, and thence to the Midlands and to the North. This synergy was strengthened, in 1861, by the leasing, and then, in 1866, by the outright acquisition, by the LNWR of the MT&AR; and, in 1875, by the vesting in the LNWR of the Sirhowy Railway.

And third, from 1868, and by means of the series of contiguous lines (collectively known as the Central Wales Railway) extending south-westwards from Craven Arms, 20 miles south of Shrewsbury, the LNWR enjoyed access not only to Swansea and to Llanelly, but also to Carmarthen.

Hence the LNWR had very satisfactory connections with South and West Wales and with its seaboard, and it would have been unnecessary as well as expensive and effortful to acquire an additional route via Brecon, which would have entailed negotiations not only with the Hereford, Hay and Brecon, but also with the Mid-Wales, the Brecon and Merthyr, and the Neath and Brecon, railway companies.

Even if they had been successful, such negotiations would have produced only a duplication of what the LNWR already possessed. As it was, this abstention from attempting yet another route was to be vindicated by the freight sharing agreement reached in 1932 between the LMS and the GWR: from the more westerly parts of South Wales freight would be routed either by the Central Wales line of the LMS or along the South Wales main line of the GWR (in either case avoiding the steeply graded single line of the Neath and Brecon route), whilst the mineral traffic, by now principally coal, from the Glamorganshire and Monmouthshire Valleys could go either by the MT&AR route of the LMS to Abergavenny and to Hereford, or by the GWR main line to Newport and there turn north to reach the Welsh Border towns and beyond. One result of this concordat was that, as we shall see, the HH&BR became what in France would be called *une voie ferrée d'intérêt locale* – a rural railway line of mainly local importance.

The Midland in charge

The Midland Railway had at its command vast resources as well as abundant expertise, and, after acquiring outright the HH&BR in 1886, it set about a sensible programme of incremental improvements, which may be summed up in the word 'Midlandification'. The permanent way was upgraded, and the track layouts in some locations were improved. More satisfactory and safer methods of signalling and single line working were adopted. The earlier staff and staff-and-ticket systems for operating the line between Moorfields and Three Cocks were replaced in 1892 by the more dependable and more flexible electric train tablet system. At most of the stations, new signal boxes were installed. These were of typical Midland design, and most of the parts were pre-fabricated at Derby. The boxes were of mainly timber construction, with horizontal boarding at the lower, and vertical boarding at the upper, levels. The roofs were hipped, and the deep windows had the chamfered upper corners characteristic of MR design. Access to the upper, working, floor was by means of a shallow-stepped staircase. The

Midland had no difficulty in complying with the new requirements of the Regulation of Railways Act 1889, which required, amongst other safety measures, a high standard of signalling and of interlocking of signals and points.

Not all of the boxes were long lived. At Glasbury, for example, the box was dismantled in 1892, and replaced by a ground frame. Eardisley West box became redundant in 1925. Such, however, was the quality of the workmanship and of the materials of the remaining boxes that many of them remained in use until the line was closed.

The original station buildings (described in Chapter 3) were left largely intact, but platform and other furniture and features of typical MR design were gradually added – for example, the characteristic diagonal wooden fencing, station nameboards, barrows, seats and lamps, although after the Grouping many of the last named were replaced by the oil lamps of LNWR design which became standard on LMS wayside and branch line stations. These LNWR lamps were well suited to attachment to walls, but perhaps looked rather less at home when placed on the short and slender MR lamp-posts which had originally supported graceful four-sided glass lanterns.

The platform lamp nearer to the Glasbury-on-Wye station building is of MR origin, whilst that on the right of the picture is of LNWR design, and has been attached a little incongruously to a typical MR lamp-post. The hut on the left of the line (and at the left-hand side of the picture) contains the ground frame, which (eventually) succeeded a signal box which was abolished in 1892. Looking east, towards Hereford   *Author's collection*

Access to Barrs Court Station

A major event took place at the beginning of 1893. For several years the administrations of the railways serving Hereford had been contemplating the concentration of all passenger and parcels traffic at Barrs Court station, on the *east* side of the city, and the consequential closure of Barton station, on the *west* side of the city. Such a step would, it was thought, result in a substantial reduction of working costs as well as in an increase of convenience to passengers who needed to change trains in Hereford.

This proposal clearly affected the MR's operation of the service over the HH&BR, and it was made feasible by two additions to the infrastructure, one new and one restored. Whereas access from the HH&BR line to Barrs Court had entailed two reversals – the first at the junction (near Moorfields) to the north of Barton station, and the second at Barrs Court Junction (originally named Barton Junction) – there was now a requirement for an uninterrupted route which HH&BR line trains could follow if they were to run directly to and from Barrs Court. This was achieved by opening one new section of railway, and by re-opening another section which had been partly completed but had been for long abandoned.

The west side exterior of Barrs Court station. Note the charming Midland Railway Express Parcels Traffic van in the approach road.   *John Alsop collection*

The first, and new, section took the form of a west to east chord, or connecting curve, running between the HH&BR and the Worcester Mile. This curve, in effect a loop line, had in fact been proposed as long previously as 1863, and indeed it would appear that some preliminary constructional work had been started but had been halted in 1865. It was now, in 1892, built anew from a western point, to be called Moorfields Junction, on the HH&BR line, to a junction with the Worcester Mile, and it was known (very) variously as the Midland Loop, the Widemarsh Loop, the Midland Curve, the Moorfields Loop, the Hereford Junction, and also – perhaps misleadingly – as the Barton Curve, and – not very informatively – as the north fork. The length of the loop was 36 chains. Much of the work was carried out by the Midland, but the final section (of 12 chains) at the eastern end, and the junction with the Worcester Mile, were constructed by the Great Western, who recovered the costs from the Midland. This connection enabled trains from Brecon and Hay to face north as they joined the Worcester Mile, over which they ran for a short distance as far as Barton and Brecon Curve Junction, where they diverged eastwards.

The second section began at this Barton and Brecon Curve Junction, and was constituted by the restoration and upgrading of the loop line, which was known as the Brecon Curve, and which, as we have seen, had been both partly completed and quickly abandoned in 1870. The works were carried out jointly by the Great Western and London and North Western Railways, who were the joint owners of the Shrewsbury and Hereford line, which ran into Barrs Court. The rehabilitated connecting line was 18 chains long and described a sharp curve between Barton and Brecon Curve Junction, situated on the Worcester Mile, and Brecon Curve Junction, where it joined the Shrewsbury and Hereford line at a point 30 chains north of Barrs Court station. The original single track was replaced by double track, and the restored line was properly signalled. The Midland was to pay tolls for the use of the Brecon Curve and rent for the use of Barrs Court station.

The result of these additions and improvements was that HH&BR line trains could now run directly via the Midland Loop and the Brecon Curve to Barrs Court without any reversal; and they could do so, moreover, with a saving in time and mileage. The new arrangements took effect on and from Monday 2nd January, 1893. Characteristically, the Midland took a decision to employ its own booking clerks at Barrs Court.

The forlorn, and architecturally rather fine, station at Barton was then closed. The resultant treatment of the imposing three-storey building on the east side platform illustrates, so far as conservation is concerned, the difference of approach between that of the late Victorian era and that of our own. The now redundant building was not converted into tasteful apartments, or into office suites, or into a community centre: no longer required for its original purpose, it was summarily demolished.

Aggrieved by the loss of Barton station, some inhabitants and business people living in the area on the west side of Hereford pressed for the provision of a passenger platform on the Midland Loop, but their request was declined.

Improvements

On the same day, 2nd January, 1893, when it began direct running from the HH&BR line to Barrs Court, the MR opened a handsome and commodious goods shed at Moorfields, situated on a site parallel with the Worcester Mile, and served by an upgraded version of the lane which had run to the woebegone Moorfields passenger station. Of brick construction, this new and impressive building contained a large warehouse for grain, and another for general goods, and it was provided with the most modern equipment. This new facility thus took account of the beginnings of competition from road transport, which was beginning to appear in the form of steam traction engines and trailers.

On 30th June, 1894, and also at Moorfields, a new engine shed, complete with a turntable, was opened for use by MR locomotives. This engine shed was to remain in service until 12th December, 1924, when it was closed, a measure taken in the course of a general rationalization of the LMS estate in the Hereford area.

There were numerous minor improvements and renewals along the length of the line from Hereford to Three Cocks Junction, although, further along the route to Brecon, the Midland was not in favour of a proposal made by the MWR (and later by the Cambrian Railways) to double the line between Three Cocks and Talyllyn. In 1904 the MWR was amalgamated with the Cambrian Railways, who had actually been operating most of the MWR system since 2nd April, 1888. For many years the B&MR, MWR and Cambrian Railways had been jointly operating through excursion and holiday trains between South Wales stations and Aberystwyth, and passengers from both Hereford and Brecon could join these trains at Three Cocks Junction.

From 1885 to 1905 a through carriage between Hereford and Aberystwyth was sometimes attached at Three Cocks (and vice versa), thus obviating the need for a change on this particular service. For many working people in the industrial areas of South Wales, these through trains to countryside and coast provided a revelation and a lifeline: moorlands and rivers and seaside brought refreshment to senses wearied by subterranean work, and by the spoil heaps and reeking coke ovens of the Bargoed Rhymney Valley.

The First World War

One effect of the First World War (1914 – 1918) was a sharp rise in the amount of freight traffic carried on the HH&BR. As well as a general increase in the volume of goods to be conveyed, some freight was displaced from other routes. For example, some paths on the MWR were reserved for trains carrying high quality Welsh steam coal needed by the navy to power its ships anchored at Scapa Flow in the Orkney Islands. (The year 1913 had been, and has remained, the peak year for Welsh coal production.) The flow of freight along the HH&BR was such that, except for a pause for part of Sundays, several signal boxes along the line were open continuously, as many of the goods trains ran at night. Temporary sidings were hastily constructed at Credenhill to accommodate overspill from the munitions factory and dump situated at Rotherwas, on the south-east side of Hereford. Conversely, however, there was a nationwide decrease in the number of passenger trains run, and we have already seen that the through service between Birmingham and Swansea was discontinued at the end of 1916, a withdrawal which was to prove permanent.

The Return of Peace

The longed for return of peace did not of course bring about a reversion to pre-war conditions. The colossal waste of human life and material resources sustained during the war was irreversible. So far as the railways were concerned, the economic consequences of the war and the ensuing depressions of the 1920s and 1930s were to have lasting effects upon traffic volumes.

In addition, road transport was beginning to make inroads into the carriage both of passengers and of goods on the railways. This process quickened in urban areas, and, although the technical immaturity of many road vehicles and, in rural areas, the indifferent or poor state of many roads, hampered modal shift from the railways, the general transfer became established. Moreover, the railways were 'common carriers', which meant, broadly, that they were obliged to convey any goods which were presented to them, regardless of profitability, whereas most road transport operators could be selective, accepting only those loads which could be expected to be remunerative.

The Grouping

Under the terms of the Railways Act, 1921, the great majority of railway companies were to be amalgamated into four groups, namely the London Midland and Scottish Railway, the London and North Eastern Railway, the Great Western Railway, and the Southern Railway. These new conglomerates were idiomatically termed 'The Big Four'. (A number of joint and small companies were exempted.) In the main, this 'Grouping', as it came to be known, took effect on 1st January, 1923, although by then some amalgamations had already taken place: for example, and as we have seen, the Neath and Brecon Railway had been absorbed by the Great Western Railway in 1922.

As successor to the Midland Railway, the London Midland and Scottish Railway inherited not only the line between Hereford and its boundary with the former Cambrian Railways east of Three Cocks Junction, but also the Midland's Swansea Vale Railway. For some years after the Grouping, the LMS continued to operate the passenger and goods services between Hereford and Swansea via Brecon. In other words, no early attempt was made to reassign those services to the GWR, in whose general area the lines concerned were situated.

The inter-war years

At the end of 1930 the LMS discontinued the through passenger service to Swansea, and henceforward worked (only) the section between Hereford and Brecon, and the (separate) Swansea Vale line between Swansea and Brynamman via Ynisygeinon. These changes were to have far reaching consequences. From 1st January, 1931, the GWR took responsibility for operating the complete service between Neath and Brecon, including the Colbren Junction to Brecon section which had hitherto been worked by the Midland Railway and then by the LMS. The Colbren Junction to Ynisygeinon section ceased to be operated as a through service: the GWR ran a shuttle service between Colbren and the intermediate stations of Abercrave and Ystradgynlais (the latter, incidentally, being the second largest town in the county of Brecknock), but withdrew it in 1932, allegedly because of lack of traffic.

These changes disadvantaged HH&BR line passengers wishing to travel to Swansea: they now needed to change trains both at Brecon and at Neath; and at Neath they also needed to change stations, from Riverside to General.

More changes were to come. Under the traffic pooling agreement reached between the LMS and the GWR, through goods trains between Swansea and the Welsh Border via Brecon were also to be discontinued in 1932. Henceforward such traffic would be routed either by the GWR South Wales main line via Cardiff and Newport, where it would turn north to reach the Welsh border, or be diverted to the LMS Central Wales line, via Llandilo, Llandovery, and Llandrindod Wells, to Craven Arms, situated between Hereford and Shrewsbury on the 'North and West' line.

These alterations undoubtedly worked to the detriment of the Hereford to Brecon line. But alongside these were other tendencies, sometimes gradual but also inexorable, having unfavourable effects upon the HH&BR. Local bus services appeared: some were successful, others less so, but nearly all had the advantages of running to the centre of villages and of picking up and setting down passengers where it was convenient for them, whereas the trains could call at only a few fixed points.

Goods traffic was also reduced as road vehicles slowly became more efficient and reliable. This applied particularly to the carriage of round timber (tree trunks and branches), which had been an important source of traffic for the railway. The need to store munitions at Credenhill had ceased after the end of the First World War. Accordingly, the layout there was greatly simplified, and the signal box was closed in 1929, with the result that a single block section extended all the way from Moorfields Junction to Moorhampton station, a distance of just over 8 miles. Eardisley West signal box, which had controlled the western end of the passing loop and access to the down side sidings, was abolished in 1925, and the main connections were transferred to Eardisley Junction signal box at the eastern end of the station layout. Throughout the inter-war period, the LMS attempted to effect economies: these included what are known as efficiency savings, a coded expression for staff cuts. These applied especially to the staffing of the intermediate stations along the line.

No Halts – or Railcars

To its credit, the GWR had very early on perceived that it was necessary to take positive steps to counter the rise of road passenger transport. The first systematic – and in the event highly successful – attempt was made in 1903 when halts were provided along the (Gloucestershire) Golden Valley between Stonehouse and Chalford. Along this seven mile long section halts were provided at convenient stopping places, and eventually their number rose to seven: they were in addition to normal intermediate stations at Brimscombe and at Stroud.

Along its part of the Hereford to Brecon route, the GWR opened halts at Llangorse Lake (on 9th July, 1923), 1¼ miles east of Talyllyn Junction, and at Groesffordd (on 8th September, 1934), 2 miles east of Brecon. The GWR also provided halts on the former Mid-Wales route, for example at Marteg, at Llanfaredd, and at Llanstephan. Such halts both catered for the small local communities living in the vicinity and, being situated in areas of high landscape value, also attracted custom from new passengers who wished to take part in the inexpensive and wholesome pastime of hiking, which became so popular in the inter-war period.

The LMS did not, however, take any similar action along its line between Hereford and Three Cocks Junction. Theoretically, it might have been possible to provide halts at Yazor, close to a favourite walking area, and at Clifford, where the railway ran near the attractive village of that name, and which already had a small station on the Golden Valley line, but these opportunities were not taken.

The GWR also made much use of railcars or auto-trains, as did, to a rather lesser extent, the LMS. These consisted of one or more trailers which were hauled or propelled on alternate journeys by a locomotive which was semi-permanently attached to one of the coaches. None of the lines converging on Brecon, was, however, served by trains of this kind: perhaps the distances (for example, the 38½ miles from Hereford (Barrs Court) to Brecon) were considered to be too long for this method of operation.

The 1920s and 1930s may be broadly understood as a period of gradual decline for the HH&BR. To the factors already mentioned above may be added the slowly increasing mechanization of agriculture, and the general decrease in domestic service. These trends tended to encourage the gradual movement of rural populations to larger centres, most notably Hereford, where more secure and better paid employment might be available. Such changes were of course to the further detriment of the train services between Hereford and Brecon. The HH&BR did not, however, lack connectivity. Hereford itself offered a plenitude of other destinations; Eardisley was the junction for the line to Titley and Kington; Hay for the Golden Valley branch to Dorstone, Abbeydore and Pontrilas; Three Cocks for Builth Wells, Rhayader, Llanidloes and Moat Lane; and Talyllyn for Merthyr, Dowlais and Newport.

The Second World War

Because of the need to move service personnel and materials, the Second World War (1939 – 1945) brought some increased traffic levels, but these were not, however, on the scale of those which had obtained in the First World War, and the general intensity was lower. After the decline in the 1930s, more goods were now again being carried by rail, although this was perhaps, at least in part, a result of the petrol shortages which affected road hauliers, rather than of a real resurgence of rail transport. Two (separate) rail-connected Government warehouses for food storage were built in 1941 and in 1942 alongside the HH&BR line on the west side of Hereford.

Ambulances waiting to take ill/injured service personnel from Moorhampton station to Foxley House temporary hospital and rehabilitation centre during the Second World War.
Tony Harden collection

As we have seen, the Eardisley to Kington branch closed on 1st July, 1940, and the rails were (again) lifted for use elsewhere, although a short section was retained at the Eardisley end to serve a fuel depot and to accommodate spare coaching stock. In 1942 the mid-day passenger trains, one in each direction between Hereford and Brecon, were withdrawn as an economy measure. An unusual, and sad, new form of traffic was the conveyance of badly injured and otherwise traumatized service personnel who were on their way to the military hospital and rehabilitation centre which had been set up on the Foxley Estate, for which Moorhampton was the railhead.

Peace again ... and Nationalization

The ending of hostilities in 1945 led to a partial resumption of the pre-war state of affairs on the HH&BR. Further transfer of traffic to the roads was retarded by the maintenance of petrol rationing, which continued until 1950 (and which was briefly re-introduced at the time of the Suez crisis in 1956). The mid-day passenger services were reinstated, at first on Saturdays only, and then on all weekdays. One goods train was run daily in each direction between Hereford and Brecon. These two goods trains often crossed at Eardisley, where the crews changed over so as to return to their home depots.

A further, if indirect, detriment to the HH&BR route was to arise from the loss of the Golden Valley line between Hay and Dorstone: this closed completely on 2nd January, 1950. Hay Junction signal box was abolished by April of the same year.

The nationalization of most of the country's railways took effect on 1st January, 1948, when the assets of 'The Big Four' companies were taken into public ownership. Whereas the 1923 Grouping had been essentially a process of combining companies, the intention now was to rationalize the whole system according to geographical areas, to be known as regions. One result of this was that 'penetrating' LMS lines in South Wales would be reallocated to the Western Region (WR) in whose overall territory they were situated. The route from Three Cocks Junction to Brecon had already lain in GWR, and now WR, hands, and the former LMS Hereford to Three Cocks section was now to be transferred to the WR. A little strangely, but perhaps in expectation of the transfer, the London Midland Region (LMR) Passenger Services timetable which began on 26th September, 1949, made no mention of the Hereford and Brecon service, although the latter was at that time still the responsibility of the LMR. Meanwhile the 27th September, 1948, WR timetable already included the Hereford and Brecon line.

The formal reassignment took place on Sunday 2nd April, 1950. At first the transfer made little outward difference (and indeed shortly afterwards several of the HH&BR stations were repainted in London Midland Region colours!). Gradually, however, changes were made: WR (in most cases ex-GWR) locomotives (especially engines of the 2301 'Dean Goods' class) and WR (again often ex-GWR) passenger coaches were to be seen between Hereford and Three Cocks Junction, and there were some detailed alterations: for example, some of the old Midland station nameboards were replaced by neat new boards painted in the chocolate and cream colours of the WR, although, curiously enough, the MR practice of installing the boards at an angle to the platforms was to some extent perpetuated. On 13th June,1955, Hay station was renamed 'Hay-on-Wye', to reflect a decision which the local authority had taken years before, in 1947, in the hope of attracting tourists to the town.

The ICI Trains

In the same year, 1955, there was for the HH&B an unexpected and notable development arising from the discontinuation, on 22nd November, 1954, of through goods traffic on the Merthyr, Tredegar and Abergavenny line. This had been the route taken for trains of tank wagons containing liquid ammonia which Imperial Chemical Industries (ICI) produced at its plant at Dowlais and which was required at Haverton Hill (near Stockton-on-Tees), where another large ICI plant, Billingham, used the ammonia in the production of fertiliser. It was decided that the liquid ammonia trains should be re-routed via the ex-B&MR and MWR lines to Three Cocks, and then travel via the HH&BR to Hereford, for their onward journey to Teesside. The trains, which ran almost daily, were a welcome addition to traffic between Three Cocks and Hereford. They ran until December 1960, when they were once more re-routed: they again ran over the B&MR, but this time southwards to Maesycwmmer Junction, where they were diverted to the Taff Vale Extension to Pontypool Road. Here the ICI trains joined the NA&HR line, to run northwards to Hereford and beyond. This change of route resulted in a severe loss to the Hereford and Brecon line.

Closure

The Brecon lines did not have occasion to await the publication in March 1963, of Dr Richard Beeching's report *The Reshaping of British Railways*, for by the end of 1962 all passenger services into the county town of Brecknock had ceased. From the mid-1950s onwards the Western Region had been intent on closing not only unremunerative secondary and branch lines, but also what it saw as minor stations along main lines. This grievous approach knew no clemency, and in the face of this policy the Brecon lines had no chance of survival.

The Neath and Brecon line was closed on and from Monday 15th October, 1962, and the other passenger services into Brecon ran for the last time on Saturday 29th December, 1962. At the same time, goods traffic ceased to be dealt with at Moorhampton, Kinnersley, Whitney-on-Wye, Glasbury-on-Wye, Three Cocks Junction, Talgarth, and Talyllyn Junction (Trefeinon had already been closed to freight from 1st April, 1960). Brecon continued to be served by goods trains from Merthyr until 2nd May, 1964. Although no longer rail connected, the goods yard at Hay-on-Wye remained open as a depot until 28th September, 1964, the date on which the goods trains which had continued to run from Hereford as far as Credenhill and Eardisley (and frequently to Credenhill only) were finally withdrawn.

The very last passenger train to traverse the line from Three Cocks Junction to Hereford ran on the wintry Sunday 30th December, 1962. This was a Stephenson Locomotive Society Special which had started its journey at Moat Lane Junction and had run over the the Mid-Wales and the Brecon and Merthyr lines to Brecon. From there it returned as far as Three Cocks Junction, and then, after dark, travelled over the HH&BR to Hereford, before taking the North and West line to its final destination of Shrewsbury. A few days later the countryside and its railways were covered with deep snow at the beginning of one of the most severe winters ever known, that of 1963.

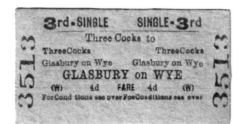

Ticket and luggage labels used on the line.

Author's collection

An extract from *Bradshaw's Railway Guide* for July 1938. The Wednesdays-only trains (8.50 am from Brecon and 5.20 pm from Hereford) were provided for passengers travelling to and from Hereford Market. The Saturdays-only train at 5.25 pm from Hay to Hereford catered for people wishing to pass the evening in the city. They could return home by the 9.20 pm train to Brecon.

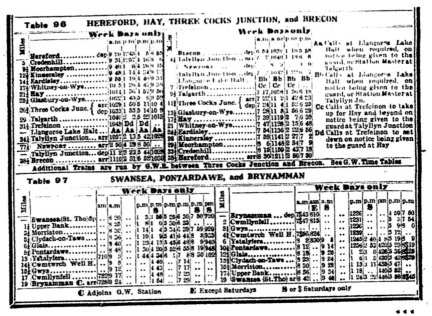

An extract from the last ever *LMS Timetable*, commencing on 6th October, 1947, less than three months before nationalization took effect on 1st January, 1948. The middle day trains (12.45 pm from Hereford and 1.10 pm from Brecon), which had been suspended during the war, and which were restored, on Saturdays only, in 1946, are now running daily. The pre-war Saturday afternoon trains from Hay, have, however, been discontinued.

Tables 144a-145-145a

Table 144a — HEREFORD, HAY, THREE COCKS JUNCTION, and BRECON

Miles		Week Days only					Miles		Week Days only			
		a.m	p.m	p.m	p.m				a.m	a.m	p.m	p.m
	Hereford............dep	9 20	1245	4 5	8 55			Brecon............dep	5 34	1033	1 10	6 5
5	Credenhill............	9 31	1257	4 16	9 9		4¾	Talyllyn Junction...arr	7 2	1043	1 19	6 13
9¼	Moorhampton............	9 40	1 6	4 26	9 15		—	Newport............dep	8 3			6 0
12¼	Kinnersley............	9 48	1 14	4 34	9 23		—	Talyllyn Junction...dep	7 3	1043	1 22	6 14
14¾	Eardisley............	9 55	1 19	4 40	9 31		—	Llangorse Lake Halt...	Bb	Bb	Bb	6 19
17¾	Whitney-on-Wye......	10 3	1 26	4 47	9 38		7	Trefeinon............	Bb	Bb	Bb	
21¼	Hay............	1014	1 36	4 57	9 50		9¼	Talgarth............	7 17	1 36	5 23	
23¼	Glasbury-on-Wye......	1023	1 45	5 6	9 59		11¼	Three Cocks Junc. { arr	7 22	11 2	1 42	6 31
25¾	Three Cocks Junc. { arr	1029	1 50	5 11	10 4			{ dep	7 24	11 4	1 45	5 55
	{ dep	1033	1 55	5 14	10 5		13¼	Glasbury-on-Wye......	7 28	11 8	1 50	6 39
29	Talgarth............	1040	2 2	5 22	1012		17¼	Hay............	7 39	1119	2 1	6 43
31¼	Trefeinon............	1045	Dd	5 35	Dd		21	Whitney-on-Wye......	7 47	1128	2 11	6 53
—	Llangorse Lake Halt...	Aa	Aa	Aa	Aa		24¼	Eardisley............	7 54	1139	2 22	7 6
34¾	Talyllyn Junction...arr	1057	2 15	5 42	1023		27	Kinnersley............	7 59	1141	2 27	7 12
77¾	121 Newport............arr	2 50	4 29	8 50			29¾	Moorhampton............	8 6	1146	2 34	7 19
—	Talyllyn Junction...dep	11 2	2 23	5 44	1025		33¾	Credenhill............	8 15	1159	2 43	7 28
38¼	Brecon............arr	1110	2 31	5 52	1033		38¾	Hereford............arr	8 50	1211	2 50	7 43

Aa Calls to take up on notice being given to the Station Master at Talgarth, and to set down on notice being given to the Guard at Talgarth. **Bb** Calls to take up for Glasbury-on-Wye and beyond on notice being given to the Station Master at Talyllyn Junction. **Dd** Calls at Trefeinon to set down on notice being given to the Guard at Talgarth.

OTHER TRAINS between Three Cocks Junction and Brecon, see Table 185

Although the Hereford, Hay and Brecon line was not formally transferred to the Western Region of British Railways until 2nd April, 1950, the *Western Region Timetable* of 27th September, 1948, inserted a new timetable 144a, to cover train times over the line. By the autumn of 1949, the line had ceased to appear in the London Midland Region timetable.

Tables 144a-145

Table 144a — HEREFORD, HAY, THREE COCKS JUNCTION, and BRECON

Miles		Week Days only					Miles		Week Days only			
		a.m	p.m S	p.m	p.m				a.m	a.m	p.m	p.m
	Hereford............dep	9 20	1242	4 5	8 55			Brecon............dep	6 50	1022	1 10	6 0
5	Credenhill............	9 31	1256	4 16	9 9		4¾	Talyllyn Junction...arr	6 59	1040	1 18	6 9
9¼	Moorhampton............	9 40	1 5	4 26	9 15		12¼	Newport............dep	7 3	8 5		
12¼	Kinnersley............	9 48	1 14	4 34	9 23		—	Talyllyn Junction...dep	7 0	1042	1 22	6 14
14¾	Eardisley............	9 55	1 19	4 40	9 31		5¼	Llangorse Lake Halt...	Bb	Bb	Bb	6 19
17¾	Whitney-on-Wye......	10 3	1 25	4 47	9 38		7	Trefeinon............	Bb	Bb	Bb	
21¼	Hay............	1014	1 36	4 57	9 50		9¼	Talgarth............	7 16	1058		
23¼	Glasbury-on-Wye......	1023	1 44	5 7	9 59		11¼	Three Cocks Junc. { arr	7 21	11 2	1 42	6 31
25¾	Three Cocks Junc. { arr	1029	1 50	5 12	10 4			{ dep	7 24	11 4	1 45	5 55
	{ dep	1033	1 54	5 17	10 5		13¼	Glasbury-on-Wye......	7 28	11 8	1 50	6 39
29	Talgarth............	1040	2 2	5 22	1012		17¼	Hay............	7 36	1119	2 1	6 43
31¼	Trefeinon............	1055	Dd	5 36	Dd		21	Whitney-on-Wye......	7 44	1128	2 13	6 53
33¼	Llangorse Lake Halt...	Aa	Aa	Aa			24¼	Eardisley............	7 51	1135	2 22	7 1
34¾	Talyllyn Junction...arr	1057	2 13	5 42	1023		26	Kinnersley............	7 56	1141	2 25	7 7
77¾	121 Newport............arr	2 45	4 29	8 50			29¾	Moorhampton............	8 3	1148	2 32	7 14
—	Talyllyn Junction...dep	11 2	2 23	5 44	1025		33¾	Credenhill............	Hh	1159	2 41	7 22
38¼	Brecon............arr	1110	2 31	5 52	1033		38¾	Hereford............arr	8 30	1211	2 50	7 43

Aa Calls to take up on notice being given to the Station Master at Talgarth, and to set down on notice being given to the Guard at Talgarth. **Bb** Calls to take up for Glasbury-on-Wye and beyond on notice being given to the Station Master at Talyllyn Junction. **Dd** Calls at Trefeinon to set down on notice being given to the Guard at Talgarth. **Hh** Calls to set down on notice to Guard at Moorhampton, and to take up on notice being given to Station Master at Credenhill. **S** Saturdays only.

LOCAL TRAINS between Three Cocks Junction and Brecon, see Table 185

By the summer of 1954, the middle day trains have again become Saturdays only. From 1955 onwards they once again ran daily, but only between Hereford and Three Cocks Junction and return.

Table 185

Table 185

MOAT LANE, LLANIDLOES, BUILTH ROAD, HEREFORD and BRECON
WEEK DAYS ONLY

Stations		
184 Whitchurch	dep	
184 Welshpool		
184 Aberystwyth		
Moat Lane Junction	dep	
Llandinam		
Dolwen		
7½ Llanidloes	arr / dep	
Tylwch Halt		
12½ Glan-yr-afon Halt		
14½ Pantydwr		
16½ St. Harmons		
19 Marteg Halt		
21½ Rhayader		
24 Doldowlod		
29 Newbridge-on-Wye F		
32½ Builth Road (Low Level)	arr / dep	
34 Builth Wells	arr / dep	
36 Llanfared Halt		
38½ Aberedw		
41½ Erwood		
43½ Llanstephan Halt		
45½ Boughrood and Llyswen		
Mls Hereford	dep	
5 Credenhill		
9½ Moorhampton		
12½ Kinnersley		
14½ Eardisley		
17½ Whitney-on-Wye		
21½ Hay-on-Wye		
25½ Glasbury-on-Wye		
48½ Three Cocks Junction	arr	
50½ Talgarth	dep	
53 Trefeinon		
54½ Llangorse Lake Halt		
56 Talyllyn Junction	arr	
76 121 Merthyr	arr	
99½ 125 Cardiff B 13i		
98½ 121 Newport		
96½ 121 Cardiff D		
Talyllyn Junction	dep	
58 Groesffordd Halt		
60 Brecon	arr	

Notations within table:
- Saturdays only
- Except Saturdays
- Saturdays only Commences 18th May, 1957
- From Newport (Table 121)
- From Pant (Table 121)
- Except Saturdays and School Holidays

aa Calls to take up on notice being given to the Station Master at Talgarth. Passengers wishing to alight must give notice to Guard at Talgarth.
B Queen Street, via Merthyr
D Queen Street, via Bargoed
E Except Saturdays
F 4½ miles to Llandrindod Wells Station
K Saturdays only and commences 18th May, 1957
N Second class only
n Arr 3 5 pm on Saturdays
rr On Saturdays only calls to set down on notice being given to Guard at Builth Wells
S Saturdays only
ss Calls to set down on notice being given to Guard at Talyllyn Junction

In the autumn of 1956, the *Western Region Timetable* of the 17th September shows that calls at some stations at the eastern end of the line

Table **185**

WEEK DAYS ONLY

Miles	Station																				
		am	am	am	am	am	am	am	am	pm	pm	pm	pm	pm	pm	pm	pm	pm	pm	pm
	184 Whitchurch ... dep																				
	184 Welshpool ...	3 15								12 35			4 30						6 506 50	
	184 Aberystwyth ...	3 40											7 18						8 45 1040	
1	Moat Lane Junction ... dep	5 45	8 30				9 45		12 50		1 30						9 26	
2	Llandinam	5 50	8 35			11 20	2 55			3 7				9 31	
5	Dolwen Halt		8 41			10 30		2 45			9 37	
7½	Llanidloes arr	6 2	8 44							9 42	
	dep	6 5	8 49								
11	Tylwch Halt					9 55		3 6		4 45		
12½	Glan-yr-afon Halt	6 24				10 0		3 13		4 50		
14½	Pantydwr					10 12		3 30		4 56		
16½	St. Harmons					10 15		3 33		5 2		
19	Marteg Halt					10 24					
21½	Rhayader	6 42				10 29		3 47		5 27		
24½	Doldowlod Halt	6 50				10 35		3 54		5 31		
29	Newbridge-on-Wye F	6 58				10 39		4 2		5 39		
32	Builth Road (Low Level)	7 6				10 46		4 10		5 44		
34½	Builth Wells arr	7 7				10 54		4 14		5 48		
	dep			9 18		11 1		4 18		5 50		
36½	Llanfaredd Halt	6 44		9 23		11 7				5 54		
38½	Aberedw			9 30		11 14		4 29		6 23		
41	Erwood	6 50		9 39		11 17		4 35		6 30		
43½	Llanstephan Halt			9 51		11 22		4 40		6 41		
45½	Boughrood and Llyswen	7 0		9 57		11 25				6 48		
48½	Three Cocks Junction arr	7 7		10 4		11 29		4 47		6 54		

Miles	Station											
	Hereford ... dep	7 9			9 2					7 35		
5	Credenhill	7 16			9 13		12 6		1 55			
9½	Moorhampton	7 22			9 22		12 12		2 1			
12½	Kinnersley	7 30			9 30		12 18					
14½	Eardisley	7 35			9 36		12 23		2 16			
17½	Whitney-on-Wye				9 44							
21½	Hay-on-Wye	10 4			10 2				2 34			
25½	Gisaburo-on-Wye arr	10 47			10 8				2 43			
48½	Three Cocks Junction ...				11 52				4 48			
50½	Talgarth											
53	Trefeinon Halt											
54½	Llangorse Lake Halt											
56	Talyllyn Junction arr											
98½	Newport 121			10 36				2 20				
96½	Cardiff D 131			10 55				2 25				
	Talyllyn Junction dep	7 47							2 30			
58	Groesffordd Halt	7 52										
60	Brecon arr	7 57										

Saturdays only · Except Saturdays · From Newport (Table 121) · From Pontsticill (Table 121) · Commences 11th May, 1963 · Except Saturdays and School Holidays

Legend

aa Calls to take up on notice being given to the Station Master at Talgarth. Passengers wishing to alight must give notice to Guard at Talgarth.

D Queen Street, via Bargoed

dd Calls if required on notice to Guard at previous stopping station or by giving hand-signal during daylight only

F 4½ miles to Llandrindod Wells Station

n On Saturdays arr 3 6 pm

P 4 minutes later on Saturdays

p pm

S Saturdays only

aaa Calls to set down on notice being given to Guard at previous stopping station

X Except Saturdays and School Holidays

The timetable of 10th September, 1962 to 16th June 1963, which was in operation at the time of the cessation of passenger services on 29th December, 1962.

Table 185—*continued*

BRECON, HEREFORD, BUILTH ROAD, LLANIDLOES and MOAT LANE

WEEK DAYS ONLY

Miles	Station		am	am	am	am	am	am	am	am	am	am	am	pm	pm	pm	pm	pm	pm	pm	pm	pm	pm	pm	pm
—	**Brecon**	dep					6 50	7 35		8 5		1025		1215		1 25		2 0	4 15	5 5	6 0	6 0	6 15	8 30	9 35
2	Groesffordd Halt							7 40		8 11		1030		1220		1 30		2 5	4 20				6 20		9 41
4	Talyllyn Junction	arr					6 59	7 45		8 16		1035		1225		1 35		2 10	4 25	5 14	6 8	6 8	6 25	8 38	9 46
—	121 Cardiff **D**	dep						To Newport (Table 121)				8 15		To Newport (Table 121)		10o 5		To Newport (Table 121)		2 33			To Newport (Table 121)	Saturdays only. Commences 18th May, 1957 To Maesycwmmer (Table 121)	6 55
—	121 Newport	"										8 3				11o15				3 0					6 55
—	125 Cardiff **B** 131	"										7T36				10o36				2 36					6 36
—	121 Merthyr	"										9§28				12§25				4§15					8§ 5
—	Talyllyn Junction	dep					7 0			8 17		1040				1 37			4 26	5 25	6 9	6 9			9 47
5½	Llangorse Lake Halt						gg			8 22		1044				1 40			4 31	kk	6 14	6 14			9 53
7	Trefeinon						gg			8 28		1050				1 46			4 36	5 35		gg			9 59
9½	Talgarth						7 16			8 37		1055				1 55			4 42	5 41	6 23	6 23			1011
11½	**Three Cocks Junction**	arr					7 21			8 42		11 2				2 1			4 47	5 46	6 29	6 29			1016
		dep					7 22			8 43		11 6	1115			2 2	2 15		4 53	5 47		6 30			1017
—	13½ Glasbury-on-Wye						7 26					11 8					2 19		4 56		Except Saturdays	6 34			
—	17½ **Hay-on-Wye**						7 36					1119					2 29		5 5			6 44			Saturdays only
—	21 Whitney-on-Wye						7 44					1128					2 37		5 14			6 53			
—	24¼ Eardisley						7 51					1136					2 44		5 21			7 1			
—	26 Kinnersley						7 56					1141					2 49		5 26						
—	29¼ Moorhampton						8 3					1148					2 56								
—	32½ Credenhill						bb					1159					3 6								
—	38½ **Hereford**	arr					8 30					1211					3 21		5 57			7 35			
14½	Boughrood and Llyswen									8 49			1120			2 7				5 53					1023
16½	Llanstephan Halt									8 54			1126			2 13			Except Saturdays	5 57		Saturdays only			1028
18¾	Erwood									9 1			1135			2 20				6 4					1036
21¼	Aberedw									9 6			1148			2 26				6 10					1042
23½	Llanfaredd Halt									9 11			1153			2 30									
25½	**Builth Wells**	arr								9 17			1158			2 34				6 19					1050
		dep				7 43			8 55				12 5		1245	2 37				6 21					
27½	**Builth Road**	arr				7 47			8 58				12 9		1249	2 40				6 25					
	(Low Level)	dep				7 48									1250	2 45				6 26					
31	Newbridge-on-Wye **F**					7 55									1258	2 53				6 34					
35½	Doldowlod					3 3									1 6	3 1				6 41					
38½	Rhayader					8 11									1 15	3 9				6 50					
41	Marteg Halt					8 19									1 21	3 15				zz					
43¾	St. Harmons					8 27									1 30	3 24				7 4					
45½	Pantydwr					8 31									1 34	3 28				7 8					
47½	Glan-yr-afon Halt					8 37									1 40	3 34				dd					
49	Tylwch Halt					8 42									1 45	3 38				7 18					
52½	**Llanidloes**	arr				8 51									1 53	3 46				7 27					
		dep	6 30	7 10	8 5	8 55					1115				1 54	3 48				7 28					
55	Dolwen		6 35	7 15	8 10	9 1					1120				1 59	3 53				7 34					
58	Llandinam		6 40	7 21	8 15	9 6					1126				2 5	3 59				7 40					
60	**Moat Lane Junction**	arr	6 45	7 25	8 20	9 12					1130				2 10	4 3				7 45					
103½	184 Aberystwyth	arr				1140					2 10				4 7					9 46					
78½	184 Welshpool	"	7 20	8 8		9 55					1217				2 55	4 59				8 38					
112½	184 Whitchurch	"	9 11			1212					2 40				4 41	7§51				1014					

o am

B Queen Street, via Merthyr

bb Calls to set down on notice to the Guard at Moorhampton and to take up on notice to the Station Master at Credenhill

D Queen Street, via Bargoed

dd Calls on Wednesdays and Saturdays

F 4½ miles to Llandrindod Wells Station

gg Calls to take up for Glasbury-on-Wye and beyond on notice being given to Station Master at Talyllyn Junction

kk Calls to take up or set down. Passengers wishing to alight must give notice to Guard at Talyllyn Junction

§ Second class only

S Saturdays only

T Change at Pontypridd

zz Calls to set down on notice being given to Guard at Rhayader

Table 185

Table 185—continued

BRECON, HEREFORD, BUILTH ROAD, LLANIDLOES and MOAT LANE
WEEK DAYS ONLY

The timetable of 10th September, 1962 to 16th June 1963.

Miles	Station											
	Brecon ... ... dep											
2	Groesffordd Halt											
4	Talyllyn Junction ... ... arr											
	[121] Cardiff D 131 ... dep											
	[121] Newport ... ... "											
	Talyllyn Junction ... dep											
5½	Llangorse Lake Halt ...											
7	Trefeinon Halt											
9½	Talgarth ... ... arr											
11½	Three Cocks Junction ... dep											
13½	Glasbury-on-Wye											
17½	Hay-on-Wye											
18½	Whitney-on-Wye											
21	Eardisley											
26	Kinnersley											
29½	Moorhampton											
32½	Credenhill											
38½	Hereford ... ... arr											
14½	Boughrood and Llyswen ...											
16½	Llanstephan Halt											
18½	Erwood											
21½	Aberedw											
23½	Llanfared Halt											
25½	Builth Wells ... ... arr											
27½	Builth Road (Low Level) ... dep											
31	Newbridge-on-Wye F ...											
35½	Doldowlod Halt											
38½	Rhayader											
41	Marteg Halt											
42½	St. Harmons											
45½	Pantydwr											
47½	Glan-yr-afon Halt											
49	Tylwch Halt											
52½	Llanidloes ... ... arr / dep											
55	Dolwen Halt											
58	Llandinam											
60	Moat Lane Junction ... arr											
103½	[184] Aberystwyth ... arr											
78½	[184] Welshpool ... "											
112½	[184] Whitchurch ... "											

Notes:

a am

bb Calls to set down on notice to the Guard at Moorhampton and to take up on notice to the Station Master at Credenhill

C On Sats, dep Talyllyn Jn. 5 21 pm, Talgarth 5 34 and arr Three Cocks Jn. 5 41 pm

D Queen Street, via Bargoed

dd Calls if required on notice to Guard at previous stopping station or by giving hand-signal during daylight only

F 4¾ miles to Llandrindod Wells Station

S Saturdays only

371

J66 WEEKDAYS

HEREFORD AND THREE COCKS JUNCTION

SINGLE LINE—Worked by Electric Train Token, Hereford, Moorfields Junction to Three Cocks Junction. Token Stations: Moorfields Junction, Moorhampton Station, Eardisley Junction. Hay-on-Wye, Three Cocks Junction
Crossing Stations: Moorhampton (for one Passenger and one Freight train, or two Freight trains), Eardisley, Hay-on-Wye, and Three Cocks Junction.

DOWN

Train columns headed **B** — *To Brecon*. The first column is a freight that "Will not run during School Holidays and is worked to Hay-on-Wye; Three Cocks Junction to Brecon." The column headed ‡—12.0 p.m. notes the working of the terminating midday train.

Mileage M	C	Station	Ruling Gradient 1 in	B (freight)	B am SX	B am	B PM	B PM	SX PM	SO PM
—	—	HEREFORD (Barrs Ct.) dep	79F			9 5	12‡44	4 5	6 55	8 55
1	0	Moorfields	245R			9 9	12 48	4 9	6 59	8 59
6	0	Credenhill	120R			9 17	12 56	4 17		
10	20	Moorhampton arr	126R			9 25	1 4	4X25		9 15
		dep	126R					4 27		
13	40	Kinnersley	55½R			9 34	1 13	4 35	7 24	9 24
15	20	Eardisley arr	102R			9 38	1 17	4 39		9 28
		dep								
18	40	Whitney-on-Wye	93R			9 40	1 18	4 41	7 29	9 32
22	20	Hay-on-Wye arr	80R			9 47	1 25	4 48	7 37	9 39
		dep		8 0		9 54	1 32	4X55	7 44	9 46
26	20	Glasbury-on-Wye	880R	8 8		9 56	1 35	5 5	7 47	9 51
27	60	THREE COCKS JN. arr	—	8 14		10 4	1 44	5 13	7 55	10 0

UP

Train columns: B = 6.50 a.m. Brecon; C = 7.0 a.m. Brecon ECS; B = 10.25 a.m. Brecon; B = midday; B = 4.15 p.m. Brecon (SX); B = 6.0 p.m. Brecon (SO).

Station	Ruling Gradient 1 in	B am (6.50)	C am SX (7.0 ECS)	B am (10.25)	B PM	SX PM (4.15)	SO PM (6.0)
THREE COCKS JN. dep	78R	7 23	7†38	11 6	2 15	4 53	6 30
Glasbury-on-Wye	112R	7 27		11 10	2 20	4 57	6 35
Hay-on-Wye arr	L	7 34	7†50	11 17	2 27	5X4	6 42
dep		7 37		11 20	2 30	5 7	6 45
Whitney-on-Wye	147R	7 45		11 29	2 38	5 15	6 54
Eardisley arr	L			11X35	2 44	5 21	7 0
dep	60R	7 52		11 37	2 45	5 22	7 2
Kinnersley		7 57		11 42	2 50	5 27	
Moorhampton arr	300R			11 48	2 56	‡—5.59	
dep		8 4		11 49	2 57		
Credenhill	245F		Z	12c 0	3 7		
Moorfields	157F	8 20		12 7	3 14	5 53	7 31
HEREFORD (Barrs Ct.) arr	—	8 30		12 13	3 21	5‡57	7 35

Z—Calls if required to set down passengers from Moorhampton, also to pick up passengers on notice to Guard at Moorhampton, also Station Master at Credenhill.

Notes: SO - Saturdays Only, SX - Saturdays Excepted, X - indicates crosses another train here, ECS - Empty Carriage Stock.

This extract from the Working Time Table operative from 9th June to 14th September, 1958, is of particular interest in that it indicates that the middle day train, the 12.44 pm (12.42 pm in the public book) did not proceed beyond Three Cocks Junction, where it terminated before forming the 2.15 pm return service to Hereford. The table also makes clear the omission of certain stops by the last trains of the day.

Chapter Two

Operating The Line

The Hereford, Hay and Brecon Railway company possessed no locomotives and, probably, no rolling stock of its own. Accordingly, the company was dependent upon other agencies to provide train services over its newly built line. When, on 24th October, 1862, the line was first opened as far as Moorhampton, the provider was the West Midland Railway, and this company continued to work the trains when the line was extended to Eardisley on 30th June, 1863. On 1st August, 1863, the WMR was amalgamated with (in effect, absorbed by) the Great Western Railway, which thereupon received responsibility for operating the trains on the Hereford and Eardisley line. When, however, in September 1864, it became possible to run trains to Brecon (reached by running powers over the newly completed MWR line from Three Cocks to Talyllyn, and thence over the already operational B&MR to Brecon), the working of the HH&BR was entrusted to Thomas Savin, who had not only taken over the construction of the line but was also already providing train services on the B&MR.

At that time it was common practice for the builders of a railway to provide, at least initially, the service over a new line, and to share the revenue with the owning company. Thomas Savin did in fact have considerable experience of such arrangements in various parts of Wales, and he had at his disposal a quite large collection of locomotives and rolling stock (although his ownership of some of the engines was not universally accepted). Passenger trains began to run all the way between Hereford and Brecon on 19th September, 1864.

This close connection of Savin with the Brecon and Merthyr Railway made it a natural development for the B&MR to take over some of the operations of the HH&BR. When the two companies were, as it was thought, amalgamated in 1865, the B&MR became responsible for the running of the Hereford and Brecon services. This continued until the amalgamation was discovered to have been flawed, whereupon the B&MR, which had its own problems – exacerbated by the financial collapse of Savin and of his enterprises in February 1866 – had to announce its withdrawal from HH&BR operations. The HH&BR Directors now sought to persuade the MWR to run the Hereford line, and, with some reluctance, the MWR agreed to do so for one year, beginning on 1st October, 1868. By now, the Midland Railway was, as we have seen, beginning to take an interest in the route of the HH&BR, and it must have been a great relief to all concerned when the MR expressed willingness to enter an operating agreement to work the HH&B as from 1st October, 1869, in succession to the MWR's stewardship of the line. At last the troubled Directors of the HH&BR seemed to have a solution to their difficulties, and could commit their charge to the thoroughly trustworthy and reliable Midland.

The Midland in charge

As was expected, the arrangements proved to be most satisfactory. The Midland was diligent in providing passenger and goods services to the towns and villages situated between Hereford and Brecon, and at the same time could begin to establish its own corridor for the remunerative carriage of passengers, and especially of freight, from Swansea and its hinterland to central England. The Neath and Brecon Railway (N&BR), whose section between Colbren Junction and Brecon was an integral part of the corridor, was initially resistant to the MR's plans, but came to realize that they would bring much needed benefits to its own business.

Passenger services

A further amenity was provided when, on 8th July, 1873, the MR began to provide through carriages between Birmingham and Brecon. These formed part of the regular trains which ran over the MR's own Birmingham to Gloucester main line as far as Stoke Works (south of Bromsgrove), where they diverged on to the GWR line which, just before Droitwich Spa station, joined the GWR main line from Birmingham via Kidderminster. They then ran into Worcester (Shrub Hill) station, where the Brecon portion was detached, and was worked forward by a GWR train to Hereford (Barrs Court). Here the through carriages were uncoupled, and taken by a Midland shunting engine (for some years an 0-4-2 tank locomotive, No. 200A) to be attached to another MR train at Barton, from where they could continue their journey to Brecon. (At various periods, a Midland shunting engine also operated a shuttle service (known as 'the pilot train') between Barton and Barrs Court, to ease the transfer between the two stations.) When, on and from 2nd January, 1893, the Brecon line trains began to run from and to Barrs Court, this transfer process was simplified: the portion from Birmingham was detached at Barrs Court from the incoming GWR train and then placed at the head of the waiting Brecon line train. Corresponding arrangements obtained in the reverse direction.

So successful were the MR's operations that in 1874 Parliament empowered the Midland to convert its working agreement with the HH&BR into a lease of the line. A logical step from this consolidation was for the Midland's Birmingham to Brecon carriages to continue all the way to Swansea, where they terminated at St Thomas's station. This extended service was introduced on Monday 2nd July, 1877. It was convenient, but not quick. In its early years (it was started in 1897) *The Railway Magazine* was, presumably in the hope of some return favours, normally deferential towards railway management, but, in the June 1906, issue, permitted itself some mildly critical remarks about the speeds achieved between Birmingham and Brecon: the fastest time for the 94 miles was 4 hours and 15 minutes (about 22 mph) and the slowest 6 hours and 10 minutes (about 15 mph). The end-to-end times of the trains proceeding to Swansea were hardly quicker, but it must be stated that the trains concerned called at most intermediate stations and had long 'dwell times' at Worcester and, or, at Hereford. At least the passenger who was not pressed for time, and who wished to avert a change of trains, could unwind in the comfort of a Midland bogie carriage and enjoy the often beautiful scenery.

Eardisley station looking west from overbridge, late 1880s. A Great Western train in the down platform. It seems to be a posed picture, with a large number of staff looking on.
Tony Harden collection

The Birmingham to Swansea through service was suspended at the end of 1916, and was never resumed. The Hereford to Swansea service did, however, survive into LMS days, and continued until Wednesday 31st December, 1930, when it too was withdrawn, again never to be restored. From then on the service between Hereford and Brecon was treated as an independent entity, although, as already observed, it did not lack connectivity, and some attempts were made to secure reasonably good connections at the intermediate junctions of Eardisley, Hay, Three Cocks, and Talyllyn.

The pattern of passenger services on the Hereford to Brecon section itself remained remarkably constant and indeed continued almost unchanged up to the time of closure at the end of 1962. It consisted essentially of four trains (in some years, five) in each direction between the two termini, and to these were added, in some years, certain extra services, such as an additional train each way on Wednesdays for the benefit of those attending Hereford Market, and an extra train from Hay to Hereford on Saturday afternoons (and a later departure time for the last train of the day for the return to Hay) for those seeking the delectations of the city. There was also, in some years, an unadvertised train leaving Hay at, or soon after, 8.00 am in term time and conveying children to schools in Hereford. This working is described in more detail below.

Locomotive No. 2275 of the Great Western Railway's '2251' class draws into Hay station with a train from Brecon on the 4.15 pm service to Hereford. Its sister locomotive No. 2287 makes the reverse journeywith the 4.05 pm to Brecon on the 14th September, 1956. Note the gas lamps on the platform, which were fed from Hay's gasworks. The other stations on the line were lit by oil lamps. *Oakwood collection*

The mainstay consisted, however, of the four services each way on weekdays. These left Brecon at, or about, 6.50 am, 10.25 am, 1.20 pm, and 4.15 pm on Mondays to Fridays, and 6.00 pm on Saturdays; and Hereford between 9.05 am and 9.25 am, and at, or about, 12.45 pm, 4.05 pm, and 6.55 pm on Mondays to Fridays, and 8.55 pm on Saturdays. (These are of course only specimen times: they varied over the more than 90 year existence of the railway, but the underlying pattern remained essentially the same.) Where possible, these services were dovetailed with those on the Kington, Golden Valley and Mid-Wales lines, the latter of which in turn meshed, in some cases, with trains on the Brecon and Merthyr line. Thus the sometimes somnolent junction stations at Three Cocks and at Talyllyn were liable to be galvanized by the arrival of two, or three, trains within the space of a few minutes. These events are very well described by T. B. Sands in his article 'Talyllyn – A Rural Welsh Junction', published in *The Railway Magazine* of June 1951.

By way of example, in the summer of 1938 the morning train from Hereford departed from Barrs Court at 9.25 am, and was booked to call at Eardisley at 10.00. Here it met the GWR train which had set out from Kington at 9.00 am, and, after stopping at all stations, had arrived at the junction at 9.38. Passengers and parcels were exchanged, and at 10.02, two minutes after the westbound HH&BR train had left, the GWR train departed for Kington (from where, incidentally, it then, at 10.29, began its first trip of the day to Presteign and back – an example of the intensive use of an engine and coaches). Arrangements were more complicated on Wednesdays (market day in Hereford), when an additional, 8.50 a.m, train from Brecon was booked to cross the other two trains, and to depart from Eardisley at 9.59. The GWR train was presumably placed in a refuge siding while this crossing took place.

The 9.25 from Hereford continued its journey to Hay, where the Golden Valley train which had left Pontrilas at 8.40 am was waiting, having arrived at Hay at 9.53. Again, passengers and parcels were exchanged, and the HH&BR train resumed its journey at 10.19, the Golden Valley train leaving six minutes later, at 10.25, to run back to Pontrilas.

The HH&BR train reached Three Cocks Junction at 10.34, and there provided, except on Fridays, a connecting service for the Mid-Wales line train which had arrived and terminated at Three Cocks at 10.21, having left Builth Road at 9.10 am (on Mondays this train started from Newbridge-on-Wye at 9.00 a.m; and on Fridays it ran all the way through to Brecon). On Mondays passengers in the HH&BR train could change into the 10.37 northbound Mid-Wales line train for Builth Wells, and on other days had to await the 10.50 train to reach that spa town. Lastly the HH&BR train left the junction at 10.38 to complete its run to Talyllyn Junction and to Brecon. The variations on Mondays and Fridays reflected the fact that these were the market days in Builth Wells and Brecon respectively.

During the Second World War, the middle-day trains (the 12.45 pm from Hereford and the 1.10 pm from Brecon) were withdrawn (presumably as being the most lightly used services). In 1946 they were reinstated, at first on Saturdays only, and by late 1947 they were running again on all weekdays. Curiously, however, the WR summer timetable for 1954 again showed the middle-day trains as services on Saturdays only, but from 1955 onwards they were once more running throughout the week.

Changing at Three Cocks Junction

An interesting small economy with this middle-day working was achieved in the 1950s by curtailing it at Three Cocks. This procedure was in a sense a mirror image of that described above for the termination at Three Cocks of the local train from Builth Wells (or, on Mondays, from

Looking to the island platform and station building at Three Cocks. The Hereford platform faces the camera and the Mid-Wales Railway's platforms are on the other side of the building.
Oakwood collection

Newbridge-on-Wye). The middle-day train from Hereford arrived and terminated at the junction at 1.48 pm. Here the passengers alighted and those wishing to continue their journey to Talgarth, Talyllyn and Brecon made their way to the down Mid-Wales platform, reached by way of the board crossing situated just beyond the southern ends of the platforms. They could then join the 12.30 pm ex-Builth Road (1.15 pm ex-Builth Wells) train, which called at Three Cocks from 1.47 to 1.51.

The train which had arrived from Hereford drew forward to be clear of a crossover between the two HH&BR platforms, and the engine could then propel the coaches into the Hereford line up platform. The engine uncoupled, ran back over the crossover, reversed, and then proceeded wrong line over the down HH&BR line to just beyond the points at the northern end of the Hereford line platforms. It could then set back onto the coaches standing at the up platform, and wait there in readiness for its 2.15 pm departure. Meanwhile, Hereford line bound passengers coming from the Brecon direction travelled by the 1.25 pm. Mid-Wales line service from that town, and changed at Three Cocks, where the train called from 2.3 to 2.4 before continuing its long journey to Moat Lane Junction; and they then joined the Hereford line train in good time for its departure at 2.15. For a period during 1955 to 1956, the first train of the day (9.20 am) from Hereford also terminated at Three Cocks, at 10.29. This was not a happy arrangement, since passengers wishing to continue towards Brecon had to wait 1½ hours for the Mid-Wales train (the 9.55 am from distant Moat Lane Junction) to call at Three Cocks from 12.08 to 12.09 pm From 17th September, 1956, the first train from Hereford was retimed to start of 9.05 am and continued all the way to Brecon. The 'short running' arrangements just described were more convenient for the operators than for the passengers.

Since there was no turntable at Three Cocks Junction, it was necessary for the engine of these short workings to run tender first in one (usually the up) direction. This practice was assisted by the availability of the Ivatt mogul engines (*see below*) with their tender half-cabs.

An ominous feature of the timetable was that, from the summer of 1956 onwards, some stops in the latter part of the day at the eastern end of the line were excised. Credenhill became the poor relation, with the last down train (towards Brecon) calling at 4.16 pm, and the last up train (towards Hereford) departing as early as 3.06 pm; Moorhampton fared little better. On Mondays to Fridays the afternoon up train departed from Brecon at 4.15 pm and ran non-stop from Kinnersley (departing 5.26) to Hereford, arriving there at 5.57 . From the autumn of 1956, the Saturday afternoon up train left Brecon at the later time of

6.00 pm and omitted the Kinnersley stop: in the public timetable it departed from Eardisley at 7.01, and ran non-stop to Hereford, where it was booked to arrive at 7.35, having covered the 14¼ miles from Eardisley in 34 minutes at an average speed of 25 mph. In the summer of 1961, the up afternoon train from Kinnersley was allowed 36 minutes from there to Hereford, at an average speed of 21 mph for the non-stop journey. The withdrawal of the stops at Moorhampton and at Credenhill made little difference to the time taken for the journeys, and so it cannot be said that the excision of stops at the eastern end of the line brought about appreciable time savings. Perhaps the omission of the stops concerned enabled the stations at Moorhampton and at Credenhill to be staffed for a single shift. It does, however, also seem possible that this reduction of service was part of a plan to effect a gradual run-down of the line.

By train to school

For some years, an unadvertised train (which had run empty stock from Brecon) left Hay-on-Wye at or about 8.00 am on schooldays to convey children to their places of education in Hereford. In later years, however, this working was discontinued, and the scholars were presumably accommodated on the public 6.50 am train from Brecon, which called at Hay-on-Wye from 7.34 to 7.37. There appears not to have been a special return working corresponding to the 8.00 am up train from Hay-on-Wye, and the children presumably travelled on the 4.05 pm (or thereabouts) normal service train from Hereford, to which the coaches which had formed the morning up train were probably attached.

There was also a schooldays working in the reverse direction. At 6.40 am on schooldays an engine and empty carriages left Brecon and ran to Hay-on-Wye, arriving there at 7.18. Here the engine ran round its coaches, and placed them in the down platform. This remarshalling had to be accomplished quite promptly, for the 6.50 am normal service train from Brecon was, as we have seen, due to arrive at Hay-on-Wye at 7.34 before departing for Hereford at 7.37. The down train left Hay-on-Wye at 7.55 am, and, calling at all stations, was scheduled to arrive in Brecon at 8.41. On Saturdays and during school holidays, this train to Brecon began its journey at Three Cocks at 8.08 am. The engine and carriages to work this service were attached to the 6.50 am service train from Brecon, which arrived at Three Cocks at 7.21, thus allowing ample time for the train returning to Brecon to be formed and moved to the down platform before departing at 8.08. Just as there was no specific afternoon return school service from Hereford, so there was no such service from Brecon. The schoolchildren could return to Hay-on-Wye by means of the 4.10 pm (latterly 4.15 pm) service train from Brecon to Hereford.

There was never a regular passenger service on Sundays, trains on that day being confined to occasional excursion or military specials. The latter sometimes ran at weekends to convey personnel to and from a training site at Sennybridge, for which the railhead was Devynock and Sennybridge, a station situated 8¾ miles west of Brecon on the N&BR section.

Goods trains

The Midland was as assiduous in providing local goods services as it was in attending to the needs of passengers. The goods delivered to the stations along the HH&BR included, chiefly, coal, which, in the absence of gas and of electric power, was of course required all the year round, and then lime, agricultural implements and supplies and feeding stuffs, and general goods. Goods outwards consisted largely of livestock, of timber, and of agricultural and garden produce, including seasonal items such as hay, sugar beet and soft fruits. The movement of livestock from stations east of Three Cocks Junction was mainly to and from the Hereford market, and on Wednesdays (market day in Hereford) an early morning train of cattle and other livestock vehicles was often provided.

The main freight traffic was, however, constituted by the through trains which ran from the Swansea area and traversed the MR, N&BR, B&MR, MWR, and HH&BR metals on their way to Hereford and to the rest of the country and vice versa. The principal eastbound traffic consisted of the products of the extractive industries, especially high quality coal and anthracite, but other minerals, most notably copper, sometimes in the form of ingots from the copper works at Jersey Marine, were also valued loads.

The importance which the Midland attached to this traffic may be gauged from the fact that in 1904, for example, there were up to seven goods trains daily in each direction (some running to and from Birmingham), with several running during the night (between midnight and 6.00 am), in some cases calling only at Hay to take water: evidently the MR considered that the traffic was important enough to

A general view looking west from the overbridge of Eardisley station. Note the Eassie station building on the down (left-hand) side at right angles to the platform, and on the up side the large brick-built goods shed, similar in style to those at Moorfields and at Hay.

John Alsop collection

Looking east towards Hereford past the prefabricated station building at Credenhill, again by Eassie of Gloucester. Some vans can be seen in the sidings behind the platform.

Oakwood collection

justify staffing the signal boxes in the small hours. As we have seen, the First World War brought still more goods traffic, and this time may be regarded as the zenith of the HH&BR. The end of the war brought about some reduction in the general intensity, although, while in slow decline, traffic was still considerable during the 1920s. There was, however, to be a major retrenchment when the traffic pooling agreement reached between the GWR and the LMSR resulted in the diversion, from 12th September, 1932, of much traffic away from the HH&B route. At the proverbial stroke, through freight traffic virtually disappeared from the line, which then became mainly one for local distribution. The Second World War again brought some additional goods traffic, but this increase was not nearly on the scale of that of the First World War and subsided with the return of peace. In 1955, however, came a useful, if not enormous, windfall.

The ICI trains

As already related in Chapter One, the part closure on 22nd November, 1954, of the Merthyr, Tredegar and Abergavenny line to freight traffic necessitated the choice of an alternative route for the, usually daily, trains carrying liquid ammonia produced by Imperial Chemical Industries from its plant at Dowlais to Haverton Hill on Teesside. The route selected, via the former B&MR, MWR and HH&BR lines, to Hereford, was not easy to operate, as it included the formidable gradients of the B&MR line and entailed single line working almost throughout. Nevertheless, the arrangement did, in the main, work well and continued until the traffic was diverted over the Taff Vale Extension line from Maesycwmmer Junction to Pontypool Road. While running over the B&MR, MWR and HH&BR route, the trains were usually in the care of one, and frequently two, ex-GWR pannier tanks, which had to negotiate very steep gradients, most of all, for heavily loaded trains, the 1 in 38 descent of the Seven Mile Bank from Torpantau to Talybont-on-Usk. The loaded train usually left Dowlais at about 5.00 pm (and so frequently ran in the dark), and arrived at Hereford at about 8.40 pm, and here it was handed over to a main line engine. The return train of empty wagons left Hereford daily at about 12.15 pm, ahead of the middle-day westbound passenger service, which sometimes overtook the ICI train at Hay-on-Wye, but the latter usually reached Three Cocks before being caught up by the passenger train. The motive power was usually provided by Barton shed in Hereford.

Local goods traffic again

After the regrettable loss of the ICI traffic, the goods traffic over the HH&B line once again became predominantly local. There was one goods train each way daily between Hereford and Brecon. The down train would leave Moorfields at about 10.20 am, call at all stations en route, and, usually at Eardisley, would meet the up goods train which had started from Brecon. Here the crews (but not the locomotives) would change over so as to be able to return to their home depots. Occasionally the down goods required assistance, provided by the Moorfields shunting engine, as far as Moorhampton.

In later years, just as had been the middle-day passenger service, the goods service was simplified. As did the 12.42 passenger from Hereford, the down goods terminated at Three Cocks Junction, where any wagons and vans for destinations beyond were transferred to Mid-Wales line trains to be worked forward to Talyllyn and Brecon (and vice versa). The HH&BR goods could then begin its return journey to Hereford at 2.00 pm. At Hay-on-Wye it was overtaken by the 2.15 ex-Three Cocks passenger (*see above*), and at Moorhampton it crossed the down afternoon passenger (4.05 pm ex-Hereford) to Brecon. This arrangement obviated the need for a goods train continuing to, or originating from, Brecon.

Sometimes there was also a late afternoon or an early evening goods working from Hereford to Eardisley, which might run only as far as Credenhill. At the approach to that station, the engine would uncouple from the brake van, and run forward into a siding. Under the careful control of the guard, the brake van would then run by gravity into the platform line. The engine would collect vans and wagons from Credenhill yard, draw them onto the main line, and then set back onto the brake van. The complete train was then ready for the return journey to Hereford. Occasionally the engine would propel the brake van all the way from Hereford to Credenhill.

At various times, livestock trains were run from Brecon (latterly from Eardisley only) to Hereford on Wednesdays (market days). There were special trains for sheep traffic in September.

Hay-on-Wye was the busiest station for goods traffic. It dealt with coal, fuel for the gasworks, round timber, livestock, and a a considerable amount of general merchandise. The station had, as did Eardisley, a comely and capacious goods shed of MR design. Moorhampton and Kinnersley stations had smaller, but pleasing, storage buildings of mellow red brick with cream coloured stone quoins, and pitched roofs.

After the withdrawal of passenger services on 29th December, 1962, the remaining goods trains running from Hereford served only Credenhill and Eardisley, the other stations along the line being closed completely. The goods shed at Hay-on-Wye was used as a depot for distribution of goods brought in and dispatched by road vehicles. Even these vestigial arrangements ceased on 28th September, 1964, when sadly the HH&BR ceased to play any part at all in transport communication between Hereford and Three Cocks Junction.

Motive power

Uncertainty attends the identity of the locomotives which were used in the earliest days of the HH&BR, when services were provided by the WMR (later the GWR) and then by Thomas Savin. He possessed (or purported to possess) up to 50 locomotives, which tended to be rapidly moved from one location to another in mid and south Wales, and so there may have been frequent changes as to the engines assigned to the HH&BR. It is, however, known that Savin ordered a Manning, Wardle 0-6-0 saddle tank engine in 1862 or in 1863 for use on the new Hereford line. This engine was at first named *Hereford*, but in 1868 or in 1869 (by when the Mid-Wales Railway, and later the Midland, had taken over operation of the HH&BR) was renamed *Lady Cornelia*, perhaps in honour of the Guest family of Dowlais, for by now the engine was presumably working wholly or mainly on the B&MR. It is also likely that Savin summoned various other members of his collection of locomotives to work both the Dowlais and the Hereford lines, and that these engines were stabled at Watton, which was in effect the B&MR's general depot in Brecon. The engines concerned may have included two Sharp, Stewart and Company 2-4-0 tender locomotives named *Usk* and *Wye*.

Definite information about the locomotives used during the course of the MWR's brief stewardship (1868 – 1869) of the HH&BR services is also lacking, but it would seem likely that some MWR-owned Kitson tender locomotives of the 0-6-0 wheel arrangement were in use on the Hereford line.

At Watton (Brecon), the locomotives assigned to work on the HH&BR naturally used the same shed as the engines which ran over the B&MR, and this arrangement continued after the Midland took over the operation of the Hereford line. The Mid-Wales (and later the Cambrian Railways) had a separate shed, also at Watton, but in 1922 this was closed by the GWR, when the motive power was, sensibly, concentrated in the former B&MR depot. The Cambrian shed was dismantled in 1934.

At the Hereford end of the route, the Midland built an engine shed in 1894 at Moorfields, and this remained in use for 30 years until 12th December, 1924, when its occupants were transferred to the former London and North Western Railway shed, situated to the north of Barrs Court station. This LNWR shed was in turn closed on 4th July, 1938, whereupon the HH&BR line engines were moved to the GWR Hereford (Barton) shed, which lay on the western side of the line (part of the original Newport, Abergavenny and Hereford route) which ran from Redhill Junction to Barrs Court Junction. It will thus be seen that the GWR hosted (presumably for a consideration!) the LMS engines at each end of the HH&BR. Barton shed itself closed on 2nd November, 1964, shortly after the intermittent goods trains to Eardisley had ceased to run.

The Midland had allocated tank engines to the HH&BR. This was in fact in accordance with general practice on the railways of South Wales: the greater adhesion and brake power of tank engines in comparison with tender engines were advantageous on steeply graded lines, and these properties were especially useful on the stiff gradients encountered on the line between Brecon and Colbren Junction once MR trains had begun to run throughout from Hereford to Swansea. Johnson 0-4-4 tank locomotives were particularly satisfactory for the purposes of the Hereford to Swansea lines, and Midland engines, both tank and tender, of the 0-6-0 wheel arrangement were also found to be suitable. The crews of tank engines were especially careful to maintain water levels: between Hereford and Brecon only Hay and Talgarth had water cranes; and those (of Cambrian pattern) at Talgarth were stiff and difficult to operate, the combined efforts of fireman and driver being required to obtain any water.

A consequence of the formation of the London Midland and Scottish Railway at the Grouping (which took effect on 1st January, 1923) was that the new organization had at its disposal a large number of locomotives of many different designs, and, over time, engines of various types were (on the 'horses for courses' principle) assigned to what were for them new lines and duties. Thus it was that London and North Western Railway 2-4-2T and 0-6-2T engines designed by Francis Webb gradually supplanted (in 1928/1929) the Midland 0-4-4T locomotives which had served the line so well; and these ex-LNWR locomotives were in turn succeeded (in most cases from 1933 onwards) by former Lancashire and Yorkshire Railway (L&YR) tender engines of the 0-6-0 wheel arrangement designed by John Aspinall, and by some very similar but slightly more powerful locomotives designed by George Hughes: all these for many years remained quietly successful.

'Dean Goods' class engine No. 2349 heading an up passenger train at Eardisley station, 15th
September, 1949. *Author's collection*

Ex- GWR pannier tank '57xx' class No. 3789 waiting to leave Three Cocks Junction with a
train for Brecon, *c*. 1960. *Lens of Sutton Association*

Under the LMS power classification scheme, these L&YR engines were designated '2F' or '3F' (that is, they were considered as being primarily suited to relatively light, or moderately paced, freight trains), but in practice they were also perfectly capable of hauling the three- or four-coach passenger trains which were the normal load on the HH&BR line. In the course of their lives, certain of the locomotives (for example, No. 12131 and No. 12428) were fitted with Belpaire fireboxes and extended smoke boxes, which lent to the engines a pleasingly eager appearance. The engines which had originated from the L&YR were later joined by others, also of the 0-6-0 wheel arrangement, of Midland Railway provenance, such as '3F' locomotives of both tank and tender types, and these too proved to be suitable for HH&BR duties.

The nationalization of the railways of Britain (which took effect on 1st January, 1948) brought further changes. Specifically, GWR 'Dean Goods' 0-6-0 locomotives (the '2301' class) began to appear on HH&BR metals. With their light axle loadings, these GWR engines had for long been the mainstay of motive power on the Mid-Wales line, which had many bridges and viaducts unsuitable for heavy loads, and now they proved to be quite capable of dealing with traffic between Herefordshire and Brecknock: indeed, whilst they were quite different in 'house style' from the L&YR 0-6-0 classes, they were for practical purposes very similar to the L&YR engines in their characteristics and in their performance. GWR 0-6-0 tender engines of the '2251' class, which were quite often used on Brecon to Newport line services, also occasionally worked on the Hereford line; and, after gauge clearance tests, GWR pannier tanks of the '5700' class also infiltrated the HH&R line, and were used on both passenger and goods workings. These tank engines were not permitted to use the up and down crossover situated between the platforms at Eardisley, or certain sidings at that station. Perhaps most notably, the pannier tanks would later be normally used on the ICI trains described earlier.

A more radical change lay in store. In 1946 H. G. Ivatt had become chief mechanical engineer of the LMS, and he quickly introduced a new design of 2-6-0 ('mogul') tender locomotives for use on secondary and branch lines. The new engines were intended to, and did, replace some of the older 0-6-0 designs, such as the L&YR types described above. Ivatt's design incorporated several new features – such as easily accessible pipe work and valve gear, and a rocking grate – which made work less arduous for enginemen and shed staff alike. The engines were well liked by the crews, especially as tender first running was now more agreeable: in place of a 'storm sheet' suspended between the cab roof and the tender, a tender half-cab provided a barrier against inclement weather.

Following nationalization, a small batch of the new moguls were sent to Abergavenny, where they were found to be very satisfactory. Soon afterwards one of them, No. 46413, was successfully tried on the Brecon and Newport line, and from 1953 engines of the new class took over many of the duties on the Brecon lines, including the HH&BR route, and so displaced many of the older engines, such as the ex-L&YR and 'Dean Goods' locomotives, which had given excellent service but were by now a little outmoded. Similarly the ex-Midland '3F' engines which had been brought in as a useful interim measure became superfluous, and several were transferred to Shrewsbury. Most of the new moguls were allocated from two batches which had been constructed at Swindon, Nos. 46503 – 46514 in 1952, and Nos. 46515 – 46527 in 1953. These moguls and the ex-GWR pannier tanks then provided most of the motive power until closure of the line: on Saturday 29th December, 1962, the last public passenger train journeys from Brecon to Hereford and return were worked by pannier No. 4627.

The 2-6-2 tank engine counterparts of the Ivatt moguls do not appear to have been used on the Hereford line. Some of these tank engines were equipped for working push and pull trains, but, as has been noted, auto-trains (or, in LMS nomenclature, 'motor trains') were not used on the HH&BR or indeed on any of the Brecon lines.

The British Railways standard steam locomotives included a class of 2-6-0 locomotives which were similar to the Ivatt engines described above.

Ivatt class '2' 2-6-0 locomotive No. 46506 calls at Eardisley with the 10.25 am Brecon to Hereford train on the 6th June, 1960. The parcels van behind the engine was presumably detached at Hereford before the otherwise same train formed the 12.42 pm Hereford to Three Cocks Junction service.   *Hugh Ballantyne/Rail Photoprints*

The main visible difference was that the upper parts of the side sheets of the engine cab, and of the tender half-cab, were tapered inwards, in order to secure route availability throughout almost the entire system. One member of this class, No. 78004, built at Darlington in 1953, was allocated to the HH&BR, and frequently appeared on the line.

Throughout most of the history of the HH&B, the motive power for passenger trains was usually supplied by the Watton depot , near Brecon Free Street station, from which the earliest train of the day departed for Hereford, and to which the last train of the day returned. For a few turns, however, such as the Saturday afternoon extra up train from Hay, and the ICI trains, Hereford provided both the crews and the engines.

Passenger Rolling stock

In the early years of the line carriages and wagons were provided by the actual operators, namely and in turn, the West Midland Railway, the Great Western Railway, Thomas Savin, the Brecon and Merthyr Railway, and (between 1868 and 1869) the Mid-Wales Railway. The passenger accommodation in the coaches seems unlikely to have been of a sophisticated nature, and hence travellers probably experienced a marked improvement when, on 1st October, 1869, operation of the line was taken over by the Midland Railway, which had excellent resources and was noteworthy for its concern for passenger convenience and comfort. There was some further enhancement in 1873, when the newly introduced Birmingham to Brecon trains included in their formation some smooth riding bogie coaches with clerestory roofs. Local services usually consisted of Midland six-wheel coaches having low arc roofs.

After the Grouping, some LNWR and early LMS designs appeared on the line, and in 1934 there arrived some three-coach bogie sets of North Staffordshire Railway origin, and they remained in use for many years. These coaches had no corridors, but each pair of compartments shared a lavatory. A standard LMS six-wheel luggage van was often added to these formations. Former North Staffordshire coaches were also transferred to the Llandilo and Carmarthen line: perhaps this design of vehicles was considered especially suitable for secondary routes which were deemed to be rather too lengthy to be served by conventional non-corridor compartment coaches. Otherwise, corridor stock became common on the Hereford and Brecon line, and examples of periods I, II, and III of LMS designs all came to be seen. Most passenger trains consisted of three or (less frequently) of four coaches.

View from the footbridge of Hay station, looking west. A down train is at the platform, the clerestory-roofed carriage is (probably) the through coach from Birmingham.

Tony Harden collection

Ivatt class '2' 2-6-0 locomotive No. 46506 calls at Moorhampton with the 2.15 pm Three Cocks Junction to Hereford train on 6th June, 1960. There was no turntable or triangle at Three Cocks Junction and hence the engine is running tender first. Note the GWR/WR pattern lower quadrant signal to the left of the bridge and the LMS pattern upper quadrant bracket signal beyond the bridge. *Hugh Ballantyne/Rail Photoprints*

The transfer of the line in 1950 to the Western Region of British Railways added GWR coaches to the varied stock seen on the line. They included both Collett and Hawksworth designs, and they often ran coupled with one or more former LMS coaches. Mixed formations of this kind became common for workings centred on Brecon and Oswestry.

Goods rolling stock

As was usual throughout Britain, the wagons and vans of many different companies, and, after nationalization, regions, were to be seen on the line, although Midland and, later, LMS, vehicles naturally predominated. Robert Williams and Sons (coal and timber merchants of Hay) and the Pontithel Chemical Company possessed their own 'private owner' wagons.

Signalling

Once the line between Hereford (Moorfields) and Three Cocks Junction had been completed, the intermediate stations (with the exception of the private station of Westmoor Flag) were treated as block posts. In most cases the station platforms were by 1871 provided with small, simple, signal cabins, which accommodated the levers controlling (some of) the signals and points. Initially, however, the cabins were not interlinked telegraphically; and the levers were not interlocked: they were simply grouped together as a matter of convenience. Train control of the single line between Moorfields and Three Cocks Junction was achieved by means of the train staff, and subsequently by that of its offspring the train staff and ticket system.

Upon taking over the operation of the line, the Midland Railway had begun an incremental programme of improvements, and these included the reordering and upgrading of the signalling system. The Absolute Block System (ABS), with its concomitant the block telegraph, was introduced in stages, the first section to be thus worked being that between Kinnersley and Moorhampton. This section was installed not later than 1873. The next section was that between Credenhill and Moorhampton in 1875, and Kinnersley to Eardisley followed in 1878. Accordingly, by then a continuous but isolated section of the line, extending from Credenhill to Eardisley (approximately 9½ miles) was operated by the ABS. Lastly, in 1881, ABS was installed along the outer sections of the line, namely from Moorfields to Credenhill, and from Eardisley through Hay to Three Cocks Junction.

The Midland Railway thus anticipated the provisions of the Regulation of Railways Act, 1889, which empowered the Board of Trade to direct railway companies to take certain measures, including the adoption of 'the block system on all or any of their railways open for the public conveyance of passengers'.

A further step was taken in the summer of 1892, when the staff and ticket system was succeeded by the phased introduction of the Tyer's electric train tablet system. Tablet working was introduced between Moorfields and Credenhill and between Credenhill and Moorhampton on 19th June, 1892; between Moorhampton and Eardisley and between Eardisley and Hay on 26th June; and between Hay and Three Cocks on (probably) 3rd July. This added to the safe, efficient and economical operation of the line, and was also followed by a reduction in the number of block posts: together with their signal cabins, those at Kinnersley, at Whitney-on-the-Wye and at Glasbury-on-Wye were abolished. The cabin at Glasbury-on-Wye appears to have been retained as a store. The replacement remaining signal boxes provided were of standard Midland Railway design and the arrangements are described in the following sections. By 1937 the electric train tablet system had been succeeded by the electric train token system, but the number and length of the block sections remained unchanged until closure of the line at the end of December 1962.

Moorhampton station looking east towards Hereford, *c.* 1960. In the distance on the right is the Moorhampton signal box. The passing loop (*right*) was not available to passenger trains.

Lens of Sutton Association

Hereford

Although, properly speaking, the HH&BR line began at Moorfields, brief mention may be made of the boxes in Hereford itself which controlled the access of HH&BR trains to and from Barrs Court station. The signal box there – called simply 'Station' – was situated at the north ends of platform 3 and of the bay platform 4 at Barrs Court, and controlled all movements to the north of the station. It was of a distinctive design used on the GWR/LNWR Joint Line (the Shrewsbury and Hereford line): it had a hipped roof with wide eaves and excellent all-round visibility. Thirty chains to the north, Brecon Curve signal box – where HH&B trains diverged to traverse the Brecon Curve – was very similar to that at Barrs Court station.

The Brecon Curve joined the GWR 'Worcester Mile' at Barton and Brecon Curve Junction, where a box of GWR design, with pitched roof, was opened in 1892, in preparation for the use of the Brecon Curve on 2nd January, 1893. In 1937 this box was replaced by another box situated further to the south along the 'Worcester Mile', and closer to the divergence of the line leading to Moorfields.

Twelve chains beyond the actual point of separation, this divergent GWR line (part of the 'Midland Loop') made an end on junction, marked by a 'zero' post, with the HH&B line, and at 24 chains west of this boundary was situated Moorfields Goods Yard Signal Box, opened on 19th June, 1892 (in connection with the adoption of the tablet system) and soon (on 1st January, 1893) renamed Moorfields Junction Signal Box. It was located on the north side of the line, opposite the junction of the lines which led southwards to Moorfields Goods station, and to Barton. The new box was of typical Midland Railway design: of timber construction, with a hipped roof and shallow stepped external staircase, it had a narrow gallery in front of the windows on the railway side. There were 29 levers, including, latterly, 10 spares. At Moorfields Junction itself, situated four chains beyond the Junction Box, the double track became single for the section leading to Credenhill.

Credenhill

The history of the signalling arrangements at Credenhill is complicated. In 1912 the Midland pattern signal box, dating from 3rd November, 1891, and situated three chains to the east of the single platform and on the south side of the line, had 12 levers (including a closing lever and

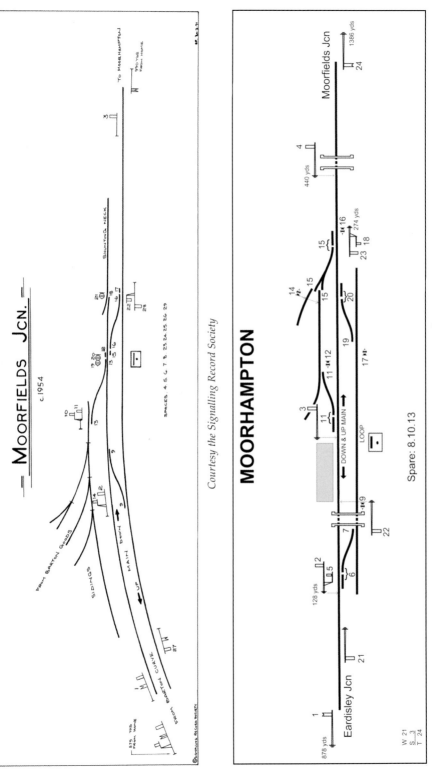

MOORFIELDS JCN.

c.1954

Courtesy the Signalling Record Society

MOORHAMPTON

Spare: 8.10.13

Drawn by S.D. Johnson from the collection of J. Hinson

two spares) and controlled the up and down signals relating to the running line, and access to the simple two road goods yard. On 25th May, 1911, the frame had been modified to enable the box to be switched out. The box was located at 4 miles and 7 chains from the zero boundary, and thus at 3 miles and 63 chains from Moorfields Junction signal box; and the distance between Credenhill and Moorhampton station signal boxes was 4 miles and 23 chains. Hence, when Credenhill box was switched out, the resultant 'long section' between Moorfields Junction signal box and Moorhampton station signal box measured 8 miles and 6 chains. This was the longest block section on the HH&BR.

During the First World War, some radical changes were made at Credenhill. A passing loop (but no additional platform) was added on the south side of the station, and the connections to the goods yard were made more elaborate. On 8th April, 1917, the 12-lever 1891 signal box was replaced by a larger box having 28 levers (three were spare), although it did not until 1922 include the switching-out facility enjoyed by its predecessor. Although it was considerably larger, the new box did not control the points leading to the Ordnance overspill sidings (War Department). Access to those sidings was controlled by a ground frame situated to the east of the station area, and released by the Moorfields Junction to Credenhill tablet. This method of release applied to other ground frames along the line.

Credenhill in 1933, taken after it had reverted to being a wayside station, following the removal of the First World War paraphernalia. The passing loop and elaborate trackwork were lifted in 1927, and the signal box (which stood on the right-hand side of the track in this picture) was abolished in 1929.   *John Alsop collection*

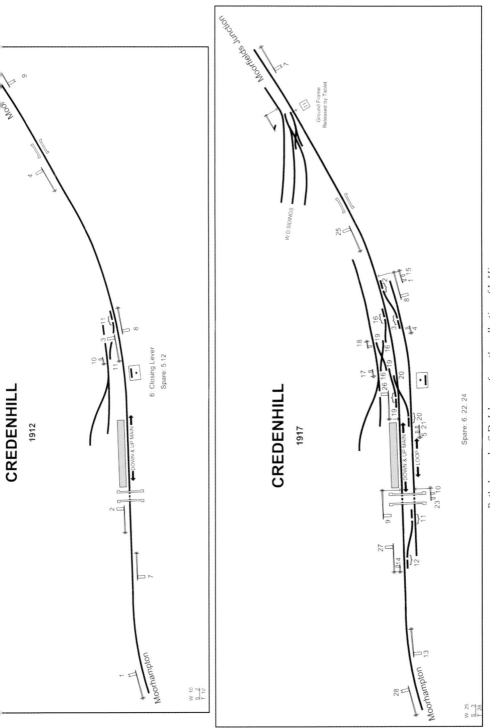

Both drawn by S.D. Johnson from the collection of J. Hinson

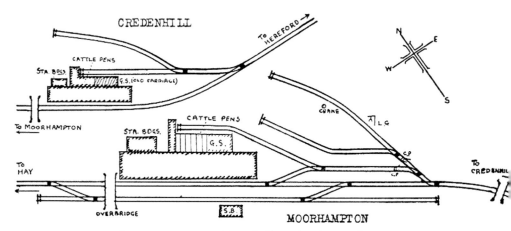

L.M.S. (late Midland Rly.) Hereford to Hay and Three Cocks branch.

Plans of Credenhill and Moorhampton stations.   *Author's collection*

With the return of peace, the complex layout at Credenhill was no longer needed, and on 22nd February, 1927, the passing loop was taken out out use, and the trackwork much simplified: as a result of these steps, the layout reverted almost exactly to what it had been in 1912. The 1917 signal box was closed on 26th May, 1929, and from then on the once optional 'long section' of more than eight miles between Moorfields Junction and Moorhampton Station signal box became permanent. There were no signals at the Pontithel Chemical Company siding (4 miles and 47 chains from zero; at Kenchester level crossing (4 miles and 55 chains); or at Westmoor Flag private station (6 miles and 66 chains).

Moorhampton and Kinnersley

By comparison with those at Credenhill, the signalling arrangements which obtained at Moorhampton were quite straightforward and seem to have changed little over the years.

The Midland box – named 'Moorhampton Station' – was opened on 17th January, 1892, and was situated 8 miles and 30 chains from zero, on the south side of the line, and three chains east of the single platform station. The inclusion of the word 'Station' might be regarded as unnecessary: the designation was, however, perhaps added to help to distinguish the box here from the slightly similarly named box at Moorfields Junction. The box at Moorhampton contained 24 levers (including 3 spares) and controlled the running line signals in both directions; the passing loop, which enabled one passenger train and one goods train, or two goods trains, to cross; and access to the sidings (located on the north side of the line). The signals governing entry (in either direction) to the loop were bracketed.

The signal box at Kinnersley (11 miles and 57 chains) was opened by the end of 1875, but was closed on 26th June, 1892, when electric train tablet working was established between Moorhampton and Eardisley. Thereafter access to the loop at the station was controlled from ground frames, situated at the entry points at each end. Since Kinnersley station was no longer a block post, trains were not permitted to cross there. A consequence was that when eastbound trains were divided there to assist the ascent of the bank to Moorhampton the section between the latter and Eardisley was apt to be blocked for a considerable time, and so to present difficulties for overall timekeeping on the line. This is of course an inherent disadvantage of single track railways such as the HH&BR.

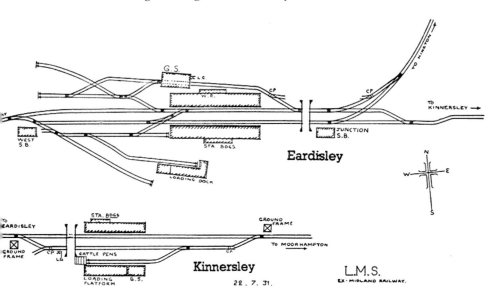

Plans of Eardisley and Kinnersley stations.   *Author's collection*

Eardisley Junction and Eardisley West; and Whitney-on-Wye

At Eardisley Junction a signal box was provided not later than the end of 1875 to control the junction with the line coming from Kington and Titley Junction. A new box of Midland design opened on 18th June, 1893 at 13 miles and 38 chains from zero. When Eardisley West box was closed in 1925, the Junction Box assumed responsibility for the whole of the station site. For this purpose the box had 37 levers, only two of which appear to have been spares.

Situated on the south side of the line, and opened on 10th September, 1888, Eardisley West (13 miles and 62 chains) was a small box, and of its eight levers two were spares. The box controlled the points at the west end of the station's main loop; the up distant and up home signals; the down starting signal; and the access to the sidings on the down side at the west end of the station. In 1925, as part of its programme of rationalization, the LMS transferred to Eardisley Junction the control of these connections, and closed Eardisley West box.

A signal cabin at Whitney ('Whitney-on-the-Wye' from 4th March, 1880: 16 miles and 50 chains), was opened by the end of 1875, but on 26th June, 1892 was closed and replaced by the covered ground frame which was located at the eastern end of the station, and which controlled access to two sidings, one of which ('the long siding') ran behind the station building.

Looking east from the overbridge at Eardisley Junction, 13th August, 1932. At this double junction the line veering to the left is the GWR line to Titley Junction and Kington. The line to Hereford goes straight ahead. *John Alsop collection*

EARDISLEY WEST

1888

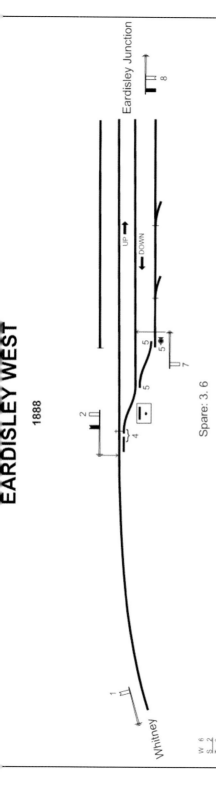

Drawn by S.D. Johnson from the collection of J. Hinson

EARDISLEY JUNCTION

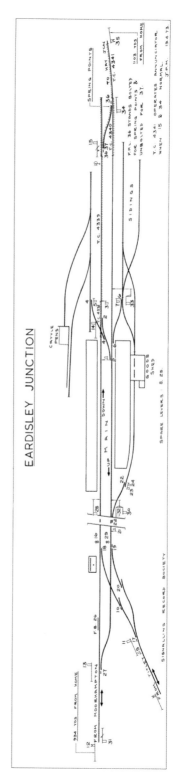

Courtesy the Signalling Record Society

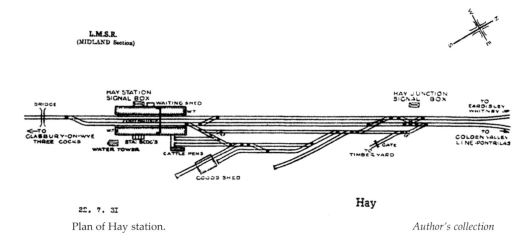

Plan of Hay station.   *Author's collection*

Hay Junction and Hay Station

The extension of the Golden Valley Railway from Dorstone to Hay in 1889 entailed the formation of a junction with the HH&BR line, 20 miles and 19 chains from zero, and 23 chains east of Hay station (24 chains east of the Station signal box). The section between the junction and the station was worked as a double line, and a signal box of Midland design was provided at 20 miles and 17 chains, east of the junction itself (which at first took the form of a scissors crossover, but which was later altered to two separate crossovers). The cost of the signal box and of the doubling of the line was largely borne by the GVR. Opened on 21st April, 1889, the signal box contained as many as 28 levers, of which 7 were spare. The GVR line between Dorstone and Hay was closed completely from 2nd January, 1950, and Hay Junction signal box was abolished by April of the same year.

The first signal box (opened before the end of 1875) at Hay station was situated on the down (westbound) side, but on 12th November, 1888, it was replaced by a new box which stood on the up platform, at a distance of 20 miles and 43 chains from zero. The resiting of the box was probably occasioned by the imminent arrival of the Golden Valley Railway extension from Dorstone. This up side box received a new frame in August 1921, and contained 16 levers. Until its closure at the end of 1962, the box retained its name of 'Hay Station', even though Hay Junction had closed in 1950, and the station itself had been renamed 'Hay-on-Wye' in 1955.

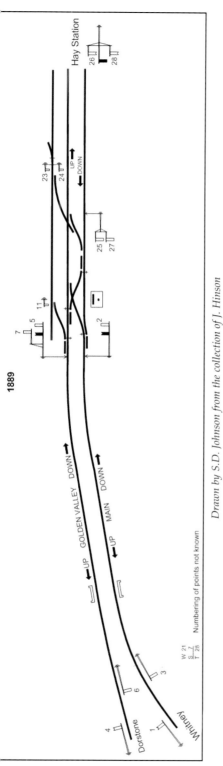

1889

Hay Station

UP GOLDEN VALLEY DOWN

UP MAIN DOWN

Whitney

Dorstone

W 21
S 7
T 28

Numbering of points not known

Drawn by S.D. Johnson from the collection of J. Hinson

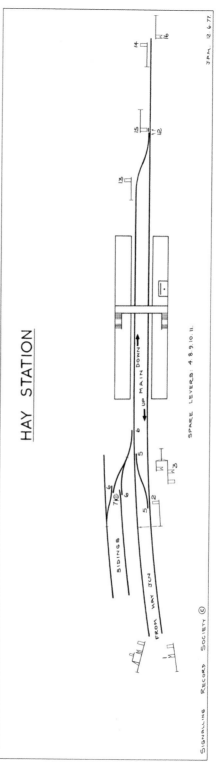

HAY STATION

UP MAIN DOWN

SIDINGS

FROM HAY JCN

SPARE LEVERS: 4 8 9 10 11.

SIGNALLING RECORD SOCIETY ©

J.P.H. 12 6 77

Courtesy the Signalling Record Society

Glasbury-on-Wye

In 1882 the Midland Railway opened a signal box at Glasbury (Glasbury-on-Wye from 1st February, 1894: 24 miles and 46 chains from zero) but, when electric tablet working was introduced in 1892, the box was closed on 3rd July, and replaced by a ground frame, contained in a small shed situated on the north side of the line, and controlling access to the sidings (situated on the south side of the line).

Three Cocks Junction

As we have seen, the metals of the Hereford, Hay and Brecon Railway ended (at 25 miles and 50 chains from zero) 29 chains east of Three Cocks Junction, and the station and signal box and signals at that Junction were of an entirely different pattern and character from those found on the HH&BR itself. The Three Cocks buildings originated with the Mid-Wales Railway, and were later maintained and in certain respects altered by the Cambrian Railways and by the GWR. Built in 1890 by Dutton and Co., the signal box (at 26 miles from zero) contained 40 levers, of which 8 were spare.

Three Cocks Junction in the snow, looking east towards Hereford.

Tony Harden collection

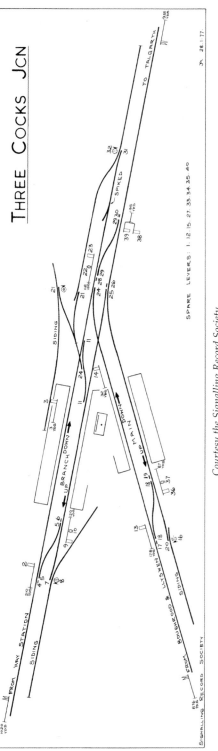

THREE COCKS JCN

FROM HAY STATION

SIDING

SIDING

BRANCH DOWN
UP

MAIN DOWN
UP

FROM BOUGHROOD & LLYSWEN

SIDING

SPIKED

TO TALGARTH

SPARE LEVERS: 1. 12. 15. 27. 33. 34. 35. 40

Courtesy the Signalling Record Society

SIGNALLING RECORD SOCIETY

The Mid-Wales Railway side of Three Cocks Junction, and
its large nameboard inviting us to change for Hereford.
Oakwood collection

THREE COCKS
CHANGE FOR
HAY & HEREFORD LINE

Signals

The Midland Railway installed signals of its own characteristic design. In common with those of almost all contemporary railways, these signals were of the lower quadrant pattern. Unlike many other railway companies, however, the MR manufactured most of its own signals, and rarely used contractors. The fronts of the home signal arms were painted Monkeaton Red (a quite dark red shade), and near the outer end of the arm was a white painted circle (instead of the more usual vertical white stripe). The diameter of these circles was slightly less than the depth of the signal arm. Distant signal arms were also painted red: the familiar yellow colour was not introduced until much later. (In 1918 the Great Central Railway was the first company to apply yellow paint to its distant signal arms.) The colour of the rear of signal arms was white, and a black circle was added to correspond with the white circle on the front of the arm. In 1906 it was decided to adopt the more conventional white stripe on the front of signal arms; and to replace Monkeaton Red with a brighter ('geranium') shade of red. These changes took time to implement, and MR 'spotted' signal arms survived for many years.

A down train gains the single line towards Glasbury. It has just entered Wales, having crossed the boundary (between Herefordshire and Brecknockshire) by means of the bridge over the Dulas Brook, which can be seen flowing into the broad River Wye. Note the circle (rather than a vertical stripe) on the rear of the signal arm near the right-hand side of the picture.

John Alsop collection

Staff at Moorhampton station.   *Lens of Sutton Association*

Of the four companies which came into being at the Grouping (on 1st January, 1923), three – the London Midland and Scottish, the London and North Eastern and the Southern Railways – all decided to adopt the upper quadrant pattern of signals. This policy was, however, again implemented slowly (and was further retarded by the Second World War), and many lower quadrant signals of all three companies remained long after nationalization took effect on 1st January, 1948. On the HH&B line, LMS, and subsequently LMR, upper quadrant signals gradually replaced some Midland lower quadrant examples.

After trials with the upper quadrant system, the GWR had, however, decided to retain the lower quadrant design for its signalling (albeit with some modernization, such as the replacement, from about 1930, of wooden by steel arms), and this policy was perpetuated by the Western Region of British Railways. Consequently, when the line between Hereford and Three Cocks Junction was transferred to the WR from 2nd April, 1950, further replacement signals were again of lower quadrant design. Thus did matters come full circle. The view of Moorhampton (*p. 69*) shows (a) the rear of a LMS bracket signal, with the upper quadrant homes governing entry from the west to the platform and to the loop, and (b) the front of a newly installed BR(WR) lower quadrant starting signal controlling access to the line west of Moorhampton.

Speed Restrictions

The entire route between Hereford and Three Cocks Junction was subject to an overall speed restriction of 45 mph (and a restriction of 40 mph applied to the continuation line from Three Cocks to Brecon). There were some further limitations at specified places. Trains traversing the Brecon Curve were limited to 10 mph, and all trains entering or leaving the down or up loops at Moorhampton, Eardisley and Hay-on-Wye were required not to exceed 15 mph. A speed restriction of 10 mph applied throughout Three Cocks Junction, including the 'L.M.R. Line' (the 'London Midland Region Line'), a term which was still current in the Working Timetable for 1962, 12 years after the transfer of the HH&BR line from the London Midland Region to the Western Region of British Railways!

Station facilities for passengers

The stations along the line offered a variety of passenger train facilities. In autumn, 1938 (to take an example), it was possible at Credenhill for members of the public to make telephone calls and to send telegrams. Moorhampton and Eardisley offered the same facilities, and in addition could load and unload horses, and could also load and unload 'carriage trucks'. (By this time, most of the 'carriages' were presumably motor vehicles.) Kinnersley dealt only with horses and other livestock, and Whitney-on-Wye did not have any arrangements at all. Hay provided for horses and carriage trucks, and also for sending luggage in advance. It was also possible here to make telephone calls (but not, apparently, to send telegrams!). The facilities at Glasbury-on-Wye were similar to those of Hay, except that that there was no provision for sending luggage in advance. To complete this assortment, Three Cocks could deal with horses and carriages, but (rather surprisingly for a junction station) did not offer telephone or telegraphic services to the public.

Chapter Three

A Journey from Hereford in Later Years

PASSENGER TRAINS for Brecon usually left from the up bay platform (4) at Hereford Barrs Court, although certain services (for example, the mid-day and mid-afternoon departures) sometimes used the up main platform (3). Because of the track layout north of the station, incoming trains from Brecon and Three Cocks Junction necessarily arrived at the island platform (1 and 2) opposite the main station building, and the coaches were then shunted to platform 4 or to platform 3 as required. Although used primarily by HH&BR line trains, platform 4 (which was informally known as 'the Salop Dock') was also used by a few trains bound for the Ludlow and Shrewsbury line. Locomotives of the 4-6-0 wheel arrangement were not permitted to use platform 4, but, since such engines were not used on the Hay and Brecon line, this restriction was inoperative.

Brecon-bound trains followed the Shrewsbury main line for some 30 chains northwards as far as Brecon Curve signal box, where they diverged to the left to traverse the Brecon Curve itself. The Curve, which, at about the middle of its course, crossed a minor road (Burcott Road) on the level, described a turn of about 135 degrees to join, by a trailing connection at Barton and Brecon Curve Junction, the line (the

The wide island platform at which trains from Brecon and Three Cocks Junction normally arrived.   *John Alsop collection*

'Worcester Mile') between Barrs Court Junction and Barton. After traversing a short section of this 'Worcester Mile', the HH&B line trains branched to the right at a facing double junction, and, from a point, where, at 12 chains from that junction, the GWR made an end-on connection with the Midland Railway (at 184 miles and 47 chains from London St Pancras [sic]), the Hereford, Hay and Brecon mileages were measured from zero.

Trains rounded a right-hand curve to reach Moorfields Junction signal box (0 miles and 24 chains), where a trailing connection came in, on the left-hand side, from Moorfields Goods station and Barton; and then Moorfields Single Line Junction itself (0 miles and 28 chains), where the double running lines became single. In the triangle thus formed was situated Moorfields Depot, which contained numerous sidings and included the Midland engine shed and turntable. This triangle also later became the site of the Bulmers Railway Centre, which was opened in 1969 and closed in 1993.

Beyond Moorfields Junction the line to Three Cocks Junction took up a generally north-west course through the western edge of Hereford and to the south of the settlement of Stretton Sugwas. Private sidings were in 1941 – 1942 installed along the north side of this length to serve two wartime Government food stores (at Grandstand Road and at Westfields), and these were not finally closed until 1964. Another siding, at 3 miles and 29 chains from zero, serving a ballast pit then owned by the railway, had closed in September 1933. Symbolically enough, the pit itself was taken over by a firm which extracted gravel for the purposes of road making and road repairs.

The line continued on gentle upward gradients and through pleasant open countryside to reach Credenhill station (4 miles and 10 chains). The redundant sidings which had served an ordnance overflow depot to the east and north of Credenhill station (*see above,* pp. 35 and 37) had been removed in 1927. A facing connection (controlled by a ground frame) led to a small two-road goods yard which included a weighbridge and which lay behind the single platform passenger station, situated on the north side of the line.

The station building was an attractive wooden structure having a low pitched roof. It was an example of the system of pre-fabricated timber buildings pioneered by William Eassie (1805 – 1861), who had in 1849 established a factory in Gloucester, and who supplied many wooden structures for railway purposes. The Credenhill building stood upon a brick base, and had a centrally placed booking hall, the platform (and only public) entrance to which was surmounted by an external clock. The three other rooms in the building provided accommodation for ladies, booking clerks and porters, and stores. A separate coach body on the platform served as a shed for parcels. A typical Midland Railway seat, with rusticated ironwork, and flower beds completed this simple and pleasing scene. In the 1950s the Western Region installed new nameboards at Credenhill and at other stations along the line. These boards were of neat design, having cream-coloured lettering on a brown background, and were mounted on posts which were, in some cases, set at an angle to the platform, and, although smaller, were thus reminiscent of the distinctive running-in nameboards of the Midland Railway.

The exit from the yard led to a minor road which crossed the line by an attractive stone built bridge immediately to the west of the station: the dimensions of this bridge, and of others along the line, indicated that the builders had contemplated the eventual provision of double track. Just beyond the bridge a private siding had been opened in 1883, serving the Pontithel chemical works, which, however, closed in 1928. The owning company had specialized in the production of charcoal and of wood tar products. The points for this siding were situated at 4 miles and 47 chains from zero. The Pontithel company had also possessed a private siding on the Mid-Wales line, situated a short distance to the south-west of Three Cocks Junction, and near the settlement of Pontithel itself: the works which it served had closed in 1911.

Credenhill station looking west, c. 1960. *Lens of Sutton Association*

Next came a level crossing (4 miles and 55 chains) over a lane to the north of the settlement of Kenchester. At 6 miles and 66 chains lay the private station of Westmoor Flag, which was built to serve the Davenport family, owners of extensive lands in the district. The single platform (on the north side of the line) was short, but it was adjoined by a substantial two-storey brick building which included a dwelling house and which was quite unlike any other station buildings along the line. Three arches along the platform elevation lent to the building an almost cloistered aspect. There were no fixed signals, and the station (which was unadvertised in the public timetables) was a request stop: intending passengers needed to hoist a flag to indicate their wishes to the driver as the train approached, whilst those desiring to alight had to inform the guard at the previous stopping station.

Continuing on gently rising gradients and passing the picturesque area of Yazor, the line crossed traces of Offa's Dyke, reached the summit (364 feet and 8 inches) of the line, and began the descent to Moorhampton. The signal box here was located on the south side of the line, and at 8 miles and 30 chains from zero. The station itself (8 miles and 33 chains) was in effect a slightly larger edition of Credenhill. There was again a single platform on the north side of the line, with an Eassie building, behind which lay a three-siding goods yard having a crane, weighbridge, and a

The platform in the picture, taken 6th June, 1960, of Westmoor Flag private station is overgrown. The neglected appearance and uncurtained windows suggest that by this time the dwelling house was no longer occupied. Ivatt class '2' No. 46506 passes with the 12.42 pm Hereford to Three Cocks Junction train. The building still stands and is now part of Flag Station Farm. *Hugh Ballantyne/Rail Photoprints*

loading gauge. Situated on the platform was a small building for parcels. It was made of mellow red brick with creamy-coloured stone quoins and had a pitched roof. Again, access to the station and yard was by way of an approach leading down from a road which crossed the line by a double line overbridge situated to the west of the platform end. This time, however, there was a passing loop enabling a passenger train to cross a goods train, or two goods train to cross each other (for two passenger trains to cross, another platform would have been required). From the goods yard were dispatched loads of high quality oak wood destined for use in the railway carriage and wagon department of the LMR at Derby.

Moorhampton itself was, and is, a tiny settlement, but, apart from its usefulness as a passing place, the station served the rather larger places of Norton Canon and of Mansell Gamage, and (although perhaps more in imagination) Sarnesfield and the well known 'black and white' village of Weobley.

Leaving Moorhampton, the railway crossed the Maddle Brook (a tributary of the River Wye), and then began to descend, at first quite steeply at 1 in 60. This bank was an obstacle to eastbound freight trains, and to surmount it a pilot or banking locomotive was in some cases required. Another possibility was to divide the train at Kinnersley, and to make the ascent with two separate portions: the engine would take the first half of the train up the incline to Moorhampton, and then return to Kinnersley to collect the other half.

Moorhampton station looking west towards Eardisley.   *Author's collection*

Kinnersley station looking east, *c.* 1960. The small goods yard was on the right and reached by the now overgrown loop line.   *Lens of Sutton Association*

Kinnersley station looking west towards Eardisley, *c.* 1960. The loop line is heavily overgrown and difficult to see. Note the LNWR lamp on a Midland Railway post.
                                                                    Author's collection

The HH&BR now reached its most northerly point, shortly before arriving at the charming station of Kinnersley (11 miles and 57 chains), whose single platform was adorned with an Eassie building on the north side of the line. Once again there was at the west end an overbridge – although this example was (at least from 1901) of the plate girder rather than of the stone arch design – spanning both the running line and a loop, access to the latter being controlled by two ground frames, one at each set of entry points. The signal box at Kinnersley had been closed on 26th June, 1892, and so the station was not a block post, and hence could not cross trains: the loop did, however, assist shunting operations in the simple goods yard on the south side of the line, where there was a small goods shed of pleasing appearance, and almost identical with the building on the platform at Moorhampton. The loop also served a cattle dock close to the overbridge. Lacking a mains water supply, Kinnersley station relied upon the delivery, by train, of fresh water in churns.

It is remarkable that Credenhill, Moorhampton and Kinnersley all had double line road overbridges, which entailed a considerable amount of earth moving, rather than level crossings. We have here an indication that the line was envisaged as an important through route on which grade separation was, far sightedly, seen to be preferable to conflicting rail and road traffic movements.

The line now ran slightly south of westwards to reach Eardisley Junction (13 miles and 38 chains), where the HH&BR line was joined, at a trailing junction, by the Kington, Titley Junction and Eardisley line of the former GWR. Immediately opposite the converging lines was Eardisley Junction signal box, which marked the western end of the block section from Moorhampton. The box was located to the east of an overbridge carrying the A4111 main road over the railway.

At 13 miles and 43 chains, Eardisley station was situated just beyond the mid-point between Hereford and Three Cocks.

The station had platforms on either side of the passing loop, with the main passenger facilities being located on the down (westbound) side. The Eassie buildings sited there were generally similar to those already described, but one part was arranged at right angles to the axis of the track and of the platform, and this lent to the whole a distinctive appearance. The buildings were later dismantled and re-erected at the new Raven Square station (opened in 1981) of the preserved Welshpool and Llanfair Railway. At 13 miles and 54 chains, beyond the western end of the platforms, the HH&BR line crossed the course of the old Hay Railway, which at this point was nearing its Eardisley terminus and its end-on junction with the Kington Railway. Behind the western end of the down platform there were several sidings and a cattle dock, and these were reached by a crossover and single slip from the main running lines, which became single as the line continued towards Whitney-on-Wye. This part of the layout was at one time controlled from Eardisley West signal box (13 miles and 62 chains), which was, however, closed in 1925, when the entire site was brought within the domain of Eardisley Junction.

On the up side platform of Eardisley station stood a small waiting shelter, which was dominated by a large and handsome brick-built goods shed similar in style to those at Moorfields and at Hay-on-Wye. This goods shed spanned a siding which had at its eastern end a trailing connection with the up running line at a point which was just to the east of the end of the up platform and which was close to the overbridge. The absence of any bay or other additional platform faces meant that careful, and ingenious, movements were required to avoid conflicting movements and delay when there were at the same time two, or sometimes three, trains within the station limits.

Appropriately for its almost mid-point location, Eardisley was the headquarters for the maintenance of the line between Moorfields and Three Cocks Junction. Some of the more unusual loads sent from Eardisley were consignments of tree bark for use in north of England tanneries.

Beyond Eardisley the line passed Winforton Wood and veered a little to the left to take up a more southerly course and to draw nearer to the River Wye. After running between Whitney village and Whitney Court, the railway entered the station of Whitney-on-Wye (16 miles and 50 chains), picturesquely situated on a ledge below hanging woods. When opened, the station was called 'Whitney'. On 4th March, 1880, it was renamed 'Whitney-on-the-Wye', and provided with an impressive running-in nameboard of typical Midland pattern. The station was again renamed on 14th July, 1924, when it became 'Whitney-on-Wye', and it retained this name until closure.

Here the single platform was situated on the south side of the line. Although still of timber construction, the station building was of a different design. In place of the standard pitched roof, it had a large and heavy hipped roof with wide, overhanging, eaves projecting on the east and north sides, that on the north side being broad enough to form a canopy over the platform. A small goods yard to the south of the platform was entered by a turnout (controlled by a ground frame) facing down trains a short distance to the east of the station. The signal box (opened by the end of 1875) was closed on 26th June, 1892. Access to the station and yard was by a short, steep, drive rising from a minor road

Looking east from Eardisley station towards the junction with the Kington line. The absence of a left-hand signal arm on the bracket signal suggests that the photograph may have been taken between 1917 and 1922, when the Kington line was temporarily closed and the track lifted.   *Author's collection*

Eardisley station looking west towards Three Cocks Junction, *c.* 1960. A rustic style Midland Railway bench is on the platform, and on the station building an LNWR pattern oil lamp. The brick-built goods shelter can be seen on the right. Note the GWR/WR pattern starting signal at the end of the down platform, and on the right the bracketed LMS/LMR pattern inner home signal near the beginning of the up platform.

Lens of Sutton Association

which passed under the railway at the eastern end of the station, and which then joined the main A438 road.

West of Whitney-on-Wye, the railway briefly ran close to this main road, which then turned sharply south to cross the River Wye by means of the Toll Bridge. The railway moved more gradually southwards, to cross first the A4153 road leading to Clyro, and then the river itself by a three-span lattice girder bridge supported on stone piers. This bridge, the most notable structure on the HH&B line, had been strengthened in 1888, and served the railway well, although flood damage to the bridge necessitated its temporary closure for a short period at the end of 1961.

Now running to the south of the Wye, the railway continued in a generally south-west direction to reach a narrow strip of land between the river and the village of Clifford, where, at 18 miles and 29 chains, there was a public level crossing. From the high ground to the south-east descended the formation of the Golden Valley Railway, which (unlike the Hereford line) had a station serving Clifford, and which joined the HH&BR at Hay Junction (20 miles and 19 chains), just before which lay (at 20 miles and 17 chains and on the northern side of the track) Hay Junction signal box. This box was abolished after the final closure of the

Whitney-on-Wye station looking west towards Hay and Three Cocks Junction, *c.* 1962. A down train departs for Brecon. Note the heavily built hipped roof and overhanging eaves of the building. The latter served as a canopy.   *Lens of Sutton Association*

Golden Valley line in 1950. The physical junction between the two railways was at first effected by a scissors crossover, and later by two separate crossovers, and the two lines ran in parallel to Hay-on-Wye passenger station (20 miles and 42 chains).

Before this station was reached, connections were made from a long loop, running alongside the down main line, to a private coal and timber yard belonging to Robert Williams and Sons, and to an extensive goods yard situated to the north and to the east of the passenger station. The centrepiece of this yard was a substantial brick-built goods shed similar in style to those situated at Moorfields and at Eardisley, and there were further sidings for the once abundant timber traffic.

The double track main lines entered Hay station (which was renamed 'Hay-on-Wye' on 13th June, 1955), beautifully situated above the south bank of the River Wye. Although the greater part of the town of Hay lay (and lies) in Brecknock (now Powys), the station was actually situated in the parish of Cusop, in Herefordshire. The two running lines continued through the station, each with its own platform (but no bays), and then almost immediately, by a bridge (at 20 miles and 45 chains), crossed the Dulas Brook, a tributary of the River Wye, and at this point the boundary between England and Wales.

The main passenger buildings, again supplied by Eassie, were larger than, but still typical of, those at other stations along the line, and were situated on the down platform, which was linked by a graceful lattice footbridge to the up platform, upon which stood a small waiting shelter, together with Hay Station signal box (at 20 miles and 43 chains). After the closure and removal of the Golden Valley line and after the ensuing closure of the Junction box, this Station signal box took over control of the entire site. A water tower was located at the south end of the down platform, and water cranes were provided at the outward end of both platforms.

After crossing the Dulas Brook, the railway became single (at 20 miles and 51 chains), and continued – mainly in sight of the river, which is here in a broad valley – on gently but steadily rising gradients past Sheephouse to reach the station of Glasbury-on-Wye (named 'Glasbury' until 1st February, 1894). Situated at 24 miles and 46 chains from zero, this station was the last station on the HH&BR proper, and, at an altitude of 340 feet and 4 inches, it was also the second highest point on the line. Most of the village of Glasbury lay on the other, western, side of the River Wye, and hence was in Radnorshire.

The platform, which stood on the south side of the line, was unusually wide, following some track realignment, including the

Hay-on-Wye station on 10th June, 1960. An Ivatt class '2' 2-6-0 locomotive No. 46506 pauses with the 4.05 pm Hereford to Brecon train. While on the up (left-hand) platform stands the 4.10 pm Brecon to Hereford train behind ex-GWR 0-6-0PT locomotive No. 3662. The signal box is named 'Hay Station' and controlled the complex layout after the closure of 'Hay Junction' signal box in 1950.   *Hugh Ballantyne/Rail Photographs*

The eastern end of Glasbury-on-Wye station taken shortly after closure on 31st December, 1962.
Oakwood collection

removal of a loop. The station had, for the last time, a neat Eassie building of the by now familiar design. A small signal box (having a pyramidal roof), which the Midland had installed after taking over the HH&BR, was closed on 3rd July, 1892, and removed on 29th November in the same year. Entry to the goods sidings, which included an end loading dock, was thereafter controlled by a ground frame housed in a small, windowed, hut situated on the north side of the railway.

Upon leaving the station the line resumed its south-westerly course, and ran gently downwards. The metals of the Hereford, Hay and Brecon Railway were now nearly at an end, for, near the village of Aberllynfi and close to an overbridge carrying the A438 main road, the line made an end-on junction – quite unnoticed by the ordinary traveller – with the former Mid-Wales Railway at a point 25 miles and 50 chains from zero and 29 chains north of Three Cocks Junction. The altitude at this meeting point was 321 feet and 3 inches. It had originally been intended to provide a facing connection from this point to the Mid Wales line east of Boughrood, thus enabling trains coming from the Hereford direction to run direct to Builth Wells and beyond, and vice versa. But, although begun, this link was never completed, and so a reversal at Three Cocks was necessary for any through movements. In the course of the 29 chains section the railway rose, briefly at a gradient of 1 in 75, and then at 1 in 264, to reach Three Cocks Junction station, at 25 miles and 79 chains from zero and 211 miles and 47 chains from St Pancras.

In its location and layout, Three Cocks Junction, named after the inn in Aberllynfi, was delightful.

Each of the single lines coming from Hereford and from Builth Wells became double on the approach to the station from the north, and they converged by a double trailing junction to the south of the station. A central platform lay in the 'V' thus formed, and upon this stood the main station building. It was of typical Mid-Wales design, consisting of a commodious two-storey station house, with, on its north side, a contiguous single-storey building containing the usual station offices, while a smaller (again, single-storey) extension to the south accommodated a privately run, and for some years licensed, refreshment room. Close to where this platform tapered to a point was a well proportioned stone signal box, which had been built by Dutton and Co. in 1890. In common with those of many other Mid-Wales stations, the platforms at Three Cocks Junction were quite low, and portable wooden steps were provided to assist passengers to alight from and to enter the carriages. An unusual feature was a small fountain situated on the down Mid-Wales platform.

A simple goods yard was situated to the south of the station, and was reached by a trailing crossover and single slip from the Hereford line platforms. The main running lines continued to the south of the station, until a facing crossover took Brecon-bound trains on to the single line leading to Talgarth and to Talyllyn Junction. The down line itself continued for a considerable distance before being joined by the goods yard loop line, and it eventually terminated at a stop block.

The station was approached by a tree-lined drive from the main Hereford to Brecon Road (A438). No footbridge was provided, and so passengers had to use board crossings to reach the platforms. The lack of any connecting bridge was repeated at Brecon (Free Street), where passengers needed to use a wooden board crossing to reach the sometimes busy island platform, upon which not even a shelter was provided. In retrospect these arrangements appear hazardous, especially in hours of darkness or in adverse weather conditions.

Each of the outer lines at Three Cocks Junction (the down Hereford and the up Mid-Wales) had its own platform; and each had a small waiting shelter. There was a profusion of name boards detailing the places for which connections could be made, when, as happened, two or even three trains arrived at the Junction within a few minutes of each other. At other times, there were long periods of stillness, broken only by the soughing of the wind in the tall trees at the north end of the station and by the distant murmur of the Afon Llynfi.

NOTE: Beyond Three Cocks Junction the Mid-Wales Railway ascended continuously – sometimes with pitches as steep as 1 in 75 – to the watershed between the valleys of the River Wye and of the River Usk. The summit was reached at Talyllyn Junction, from where the line had become the responsibility of the Brecon and Merthyr Railway, and from where the line descended to Brecon. Detailed and illustrated descriptions of the lines between Three Cocks Junction and Talyllyn Junction may be found in *The Mid-Wales Railway*, by R. W. Kidner; and between Talyllyn Junction and Brecon in *The Brecon and Merthyr Railway*, by D. S. Barrie, and revised by R. W. Kidner. Both of these books are published by the Oakwood Press (*see the Bibliography*).

Eplilogue

The closure of the railway running between Hereford and Three Cocks Junction was deeply regrettable, but almost certainly inevitable. Although he personally withdrew from the scheme, Captain Walter Devereux was probably correct in his advocacy of a mainly local line, as distinct from the grandiose schemes for through routes to west Wales, for which much talk but little money was forthcoming.

Nevertheless, the route between Hereford and Brecon was not an entirely natural one. Often mooted but never built, a line following the Usk Valley between Brecon and Abergavenny might have been more successful. As it was, the HH&BR traversed a deeply rural area, with Hay as the only intermediate town of appreciable size: otherwise the stations served only small villages and settlements, whose populations in some cases actually declined in the 20th century as agriculture gradually became less labour intensive and towns offered more attractive employment possibilities.

It was left to the Midland Railway with its strategic awareness and financial resources to take the opportunity at first to operate and then to acquire the HH&BR as a link in a through route connecting the maritime and mineral wealth of Swansea and of its hinterland with the central counties of England. This strategy worked well for some decades; and the extra traffic in wartime meant that the Hereford, Hay and Brecon Railway reached its zenith during the First World War.

Hay-on-Wye is situated on the border between England and Wales which lies just beyond the barrow crossing at the west end of the platform. *Author's collection*

Conversely, however, the withdrawal of through passenger services between Birmingham and Swansea (at the end of 1916) and between Hereford and Swansea (at the end of 1930), and, more importantly still, the re-routing, in 1932, of goods traffic away from the Midland route between Ynisygeinon and Hereford meant that the HH&BR reverted to being the local line which it had originally been. But this time there was competition in the form of road transport, which, despite its early technical inadequacies, over time came to abstract both passenger and goods traffic from the HH&B.

This process was retarded but not reversed by the Second World War. Wartime conditions not only produced their own traffic but also led to the introduction of petrol rationing, which in the event lasted until 1950 and slowed the growth of road transport. When, however, this growth did resume, so did the rundown of many rural railways.

After nationalization, which took effect on 1st January, 1948, the Hereford, Hay and Brecon line had the misfortune of falling (on 2nd April, 1950) into the hands of the Western Region of British Railways. During the second part of the 1950s and in the early 1960s this Western Region pursued a ruthless policy of closing secondary lines, branch lines, and wayside stations along main lines. This policy seems to have been applied with especial vigour and severity in the case of railways which had not belonged to the former GWR. These lines included the series of former London and South Western Railway lines in Somerset, Dorset, Devon, and Cornwall. Of Midland pedigree, the HH&BR could hope for no clemency, and indeed the Western Region had no hesitation in closing all the lines serving Brecon, thus creating a railway wilderness in mid Wales. The Brecon lines did not need to await condemnation in Dr Beeching's much censured but influential report *The Reshaping of British Railways*, published in March, 1963: by then they had already succumbed.

BIBLIOGRAPHY

Barrie, D. S. M., revised by Kidner, R. W., *The Brecon and Merthyr Railway*, second edition, The Oakwood Press, 1991.

Barrie, D. S. M., *A Regional History of the Railways of Great Britain, Volume 12, South Wales*, David and Charles, 1980.

Bartlett, S., *Hereford Locomotive Shed: Engine and Train Workings*, Pen and Sword Transport, 2017.

Baughan, P. E., *A Regional History of the Railways of Great Britain, Volume 11, North and Mid Wales*, David and Charles, 1980.

Briwnant-Jones, G., and Dunstone, D., *The Origins of the LMS in South Wales*, Gomer, 1999.

Christiansen, R., *A Regional History of the Railways of Great Britain, Volume 13, Thames and Severn*, David and Charles, 1981.

Christiansen, R., *Forgotten Railways, Volume 11, Severn Valley and Welsh Border*, David and Charles, 1988.

Christiansen, R. and Miller, R. W., *The Cambrian Railways, Volume I: 1852 -1888*, David and Charles, new edition, 1971;
— *The Cambrian Railways, Volume II: 1889 – 1968*, David and Charles, 1968.

Clinker, C. R., *The Hay Railway*, David and Charles, 1960.

Dale, P., *Herefordshire and Worcestershire's Lost Railways*, Stenlake Publishing, 2004.

Dale, P., *Brecknock, Carmarthen and Radnor's Lost Railways*, Stenlake Publishing, 2005

Dow, G., *Midland Style, Historical Model Railway Society*, 1975.

Gough, J, *The Midland Railway: A Chronology*, Railway and Canal Historical Society, 1989.

Kidner, R. W., *The Mid-Wales Railway*, The Oakwood Press, 1990.

Lowe, D. J., *The Mid Wales Line*, Book Law Publications, 2017.

Mitchell, V. and Smith, K., *Branch Lines around Hay-on-Wye*, Middleton Press, 2007.

Mitchell, V. and Smith, K., *Worcester to Hereford*, Middleton Press, 2004, reprinted 2012.

Morgan, H, *South Wales Branch Lines*, Ian Allan, 1984.

Mowat, *The Golden Valley Railway*, University of Wales Press, 1964.

Oppitz, L., *Lost Railways of Herefordshire and Worcestershire*, Countryside Books, 2002.

Page, J., *Forgotten Railways, South Wales*, David and Charles, 1979.

Rattenbury, G. and Cook, R., *The Hay and Kington Railways*, Railway and Canal Historical Society, 1996.

Rolt, L. T. C., *Lines of Character*, Branch Line Publications, revised edition, 1974.

Smith, W. H., *The Hereford, Hay and Brecon Branch*, Kidderminster Railway Museum, 2008.

Smith, W. H., *The Golden Valley Railway*, Wild Swan Publications, 1993.

Wood, G., *Railways of Hereford*, Author, in conjunction with Kidderminster Railway Museum, 2003.

Railway Magazine (*RM*) Articles (in chronological order):

Perkins, T. R., 'The Midland Railway In Wales', *RM*, 15 (1904), pp. 9 – 18.

Martin, W. P, 'Internal Cross-Country Train Connections: III – Midland Railway', *RM*, 18 (1906), pp. 147 – 155.

Hopwood, H. L., 'The Brecon and Merthyr Railway: Its History and Locomotives', *RM*, 43 (1918), pp. 73 – 85.
— 'The Midland Railway and Swansea, in The Why and the Wherefore', *RM*, 74 (1934), p.217.
— 'The Midland Railway and Swansea, in Pertinent Paragraphs', *RM*, 75 (1934), pp. 373 – 375.

Perkins, T. R., 'Railways in the Wye Valley', *RM*, 83 (1938), pp. 203 – 208; 355 – 360; and 435 -438. *N. B.*: pp. 203, 206, 357 – 360 and 435 are especially relevant.

Barnsdale, A. F. N., 'The Neath and Brecon Railway', *RM*, 85 (1939), pp. 185 – 190.

Hewitt, J. D., 'The Kington Branch of the G.W.R.', *RM*, 85 (1939), pp. 191 – 196.

Sands, T. B., 'Talyllyn – A Rural Welsh Junction', *RM* 97 (1951), pp. 361 – 366, 376 – 377, and 415. See also pp. 491 and 568 for further notes.

Clinker, C. R., 'The Railways of West Herefordshire', *RM*, 103 (1957), pp. 599 – 605.

Barrie, D. S., 'Railways to Brecon – 1', *RM*, 106 (1960), pp. 311 – 317.

Clinker, C. R., 'Railways to Brecon – 2', *RM*, 106 (1960), pp. 375 – 381 and 385.

INDEX

Entries in **bold** are illustrations.

Abergavenny 8, 10, 30, 67
Abergavenny to Brecon proposed railway 9, 101
Aberllynfi 10, 99
Admiralty 11
Agricultural traffic 8, 59
Almeley 27, 28
Barrs Court Junction 11, 15, 16, 32, 64, 88
Barrs Court station 11, 14, 17, 24, 32, **32**, 33, 34, 52, 55, 64, 87, **87**; broad gauge 15, 16, 17
Barton Junction 11, 15, 16, 32
Barton station 11, 15, 21, 23, 24, 33, 34, 52, 72; access battles 21, 24, 25
Beeching, Dr Richard 42, 102
Board of Trade 21, 71; inspections 19, 20
Bolden, Mr S. E. 24
Brecknock and Abergavenny Canal 7, 8, 21
Brecon 7, 8, 9, 11, 12, 13, 18, 21, 23, 24, 30, 34, 38, 40, 42, 51, 52, 54, 55, 56, 57, 58, 64, 67, 99
Brecon and Merthyr Tydfil Junction Railway (B&MR) 9, 10, 12, 21, 23, 24, 30, 34, 51, 54, 59, 68; amalgamation with HH&BR 22
Brecon Curve 16, 17, 33, 72, 87
Brecon, Watton depot 21, 63, 68
British Railways (see Western Region)
Brynderwen 10, 12
Brynderwen tunnel 7, 13
Builth Wells 10, 39, 56, 99
Bulmers Railway Centre 88
Burlinjobb 7, 8
Bus services 37
Cambrian Railway 34, 36, 63, 82
Central Wales Railway 10, 29
Clayton, James 15
Clifford 19, 38, 96
Coal traffic 21, 23, 29, 30, 35, 59, 62
Colbren Junction 26, 36, 37, 64
Copper industry 23, 59
Court of Chancery 22
Credenhill 35, 42, 57, 58, **60**, 62, 63, **74**, 86, 88; signal box 37, 72, 74, 76; munitions sidings 35, 37, 74; Rector of 7
Devereux, Captain Walter 8, 9, 101
Dorstone 28, 39, 40, 80
Double headed working 20, 91
Dowlais 9, 39, 41, 61, 63
Dutton and Co. 82, 99
Dulas Brook 10, 84, 97
Eardisley 7, 12, 18, 28, 38, 40, 42, 51, 58
Eardisley Junction 27, 54, 78, **78**, 93; Signal box 37, 78
Eardisley station 1, 8, 19, 20, 21, **26**, **53**, 55, **60**, 62, 63, 64, **65**, 67, 86, 93, 94, **95**, 97
Eardisley, West box 31, 78, 94
Eassie building 15, **60**, 88, 90, 93, 99
Glasbury-on-Wye 7, 12, 20, **31**, 42, 71, 86, 97, **98**; signal box 31, 82
Golden Valley Railway (GVR) 28, 38, 39, 40, 55, 80, 82, 96, 97
Gooch, Sir Daniel 24
Great Western Railway (GWR) 17, 21, 23, 24, 27, 28, 30, 33, 36, 37, 38, 51, 52, 55, 61, 63, 64, 72, 85, 88

Grouping 27, 36, 40, 64, 68, 84
Haverton Hill, Teeside 41, 61
Hay Junction 28, 54; signal box 40, 80, 96
Hay Railway 7, 8, 9, 10, 18, 19, 93
Hay station 18, 19, 20, 24, 28, 39, 40, 54, **54**, 58, 59, 68, **69**, 80, **84**, 86, 97, **98**; renamed 41, 80
Hay-on-Wye 7, 8, 18, 42
Hereford 8, 9, 11, 13, 19, 23, 30, 34, 36, 38, 39, 41, 42, 53, 54, 55, 57, 58, 61, 62, 63, 64, 72, 94, 101, 101; signal boxes 72
Hereford, Hay and Brecon Railway (HH&BR) 11, 12, 13, 16, 17, 18, 19, 22, 27, 28, 29, 51, 52, 59; amalgamation with B&MR 22; with MR 27, 30; first sod cut 18; train services 21, 22, 23, 24, 51, 63
Hereford and Gloucester Canal 16
Hereford Curve 17
Hereford, Ross and Gloucester Railway (HR&GR) 15, 16
Imperial Chemical Industries (ICI) 41, 61, 66, 68
Kington 7, 8, 27, 39, 55, 93
Kington and Eardisley Railway (K&ER) 27, 40, 93
Kington Railway 7, 8, 27, 93
Kinnersley 19, 20, 42 57, 58, 62, 71, 77, 91, **92**, 93
Lancashire and Yorkshire Railway (L&YR) 64, 65
Llandovery 10, 37
Llanelly 23, 29
Llanidloes 10, 21, 39
London and North Western Railway (LNWR) 17, 29, 33, 64
London Midland and Scottish Railway (LMS) 27, 30, 34, 36, 37, 40, 54, 61, 64, 84
London Midland Region (LMR) 40, 41, 86, 91
Market day services 44, 54, 55, 56, 59, 62
McCormick and Holme 18
Merther Tydfil 9, 29, 39, 42
Mid Wales Railway (MWR) 10, 12, 19, 20, 21, 23, 24, 30, 34, 51, 59, 63, 68
Midland (Moorfields) Loop 17, 33, 34, 72
Midland Railway (MR) 17, 23, 24, 30, 32, 33, 34, 36, 37, 51, 52, 53, 59, 63, 64, 68, 71, 84, 88, 89, 99, 101
Monmouthshire Canal 8
Moorfields station 19, 21, 23, 24, 32, 34, 62, 64, 72, 88, 94, 97
Moorhampton 19, 20, **39**, 40, 51, 57, 58, 62, **69**, **71**, 74, 76, 77, **85**, 86, 90, 92
Nationalization 40, 70, 85
Neath 26, 36, 37
Neath and Brecon Railway (N&BR) 26 30, 42 52, 59
Newbridge 10, 12, 55, 57
Newport 8, 29, 39, 67
Newport, Abergavenny and Hereford Railway (NA&HR) 12, 15, 17, 21, 29
Norton Canon 19, 91
Parton Cross 7
Penlan Farm 18

Penson, John 15
Petrol shortage 39, 40, 102
Pontithiel Chemical Company 70, 76, 8
Pontrilas 28, 39, 55
Redhill Junction 17, 64
Rhymney Railway 9
Rich, Captain 19
River Wye 7, 8, 9, 10, 11, 18, 20, 91, 94, 97; bridging 19
Road transport 34, 37, 39, 63, 102
Robert Williams & Sons 70, 97
Rolls Court 25
Rotherwas Junction 17
Rotherwas munitions factory 35
Savin, Thomas 18, 22, 51, 63, 68
Scethrog Ridge 10
School services 54, 58, 59
Sheep House Farm 11, 13
Shrewsbury 15, 29, 42 67
Shrewsbury and Hereford Railway (S&H 11, 13, 14, 15, 16, 17
Signal Boxes 12, 30, 35, 70-83
Single line working 30, 70, 71, 72, 74, 76,
Stephenson Locomotive Society 42
Stretton Sugwas 20, 88
Summit 20, 90
Sunday services 28. 35, 59
Swansea 9, 23, 26, 29, 36, 37, 52, 59, 10
Swansea Vale and Neath and Brecon Junction Railway (SV and N&BJR)
Swansea Vale Railway (SVR) 25
Talgarth 7, 42, 57, 99
Talybont 9, 10, 12
Talyllyn 12, 19
Talyllyn Junction 7, 12, 21, 34, 39, 42, 5 54, 55, 56, 57, 99
Talyllyn tunnel 13, 19
Three Cocks Junction 2, 12, 13, 20, 34, 40, 41, 42, 53, 54, 55, **56**, 56, 57, 58, 59 61, **65**, 82, **82**, **83**, 86, 99, 101; Aberllyn 10; unfinished east-west chord 12, end on junction 12, 19, 20, 36, 82, 9
Through Services Birmingham – Brecon 52, 53, 68; Birmingham – Swansea 26, 53, 54, 102; Hereford – Aberystwyth Hereford – Swansea 27, 36, 54, 102
Traherne, Thomas 7
Trefeinion 19, 42
Trevithel Court Farm 11
Tyler, Captain 20
Wales, Border 7, 10, 37; South 23, 2 29, 30, 34, 37; West 8, 9, 23, 30
Watton Wharf 7
Welshpool and Llanfair Railway 93
West Midland Railway (WMR) 12, 21, 5
Western Region (WR) 40, 41, 70, 85, 8
Westmoor Flag station 20, 70, 90, **90**
Whitney 3, 13, 19, 20, 42, 71, 78, 86, 94
Whitney Toll Bridge 11, 96
Worcester 8, 24, 52, 53
Worcester and Hereford Railway 15
Worcester Mile 15, 17, 21, 33, 34, 72, 8
Yazor 38, 90
Ynisygeinon 26, 36, 37, 102
Yolland, Captain 20